GROWFLOW COACHING

- A Mindful Approach

By Anthony Wolfe

Published by
ADP Publishing

First Published 2014
Copyright Anthony Padgett 2014

ISBN 978-0-9572919-2-8

2. *Find*	1. Goal	8. *Work*
F	**G**	*W*
3. **Reality**		7.Way Forward
R	0. GROW*FLOW*	**W**
4. *Learn*	5. **Options**	6. *Organise*
L	**O**	*O*

Dedicated to STS

INDEX

Preface

1. Introduction
Definitions of Coaching
Driving and Gardening

2. Goal Setting
Pinnacle & Balance
Mindfulness, Self1, Self2 & Self3

3. Does Coaching Develop Will or Skill?
Coach, Coachee, Will & Skill
Resistance To Coaching

4. A Coach Focusses, Expands and Delves Deep
Model T + Interference (Skill)
Deeper Levels (Will)

5. Skills For Coaching Sessions
General Coach's Skills
Directive vs Non – Directive Principles
Summary Of A Coaching Session

5a. Skills - Rapport
Some Skills Used In Creating Rapport
A Note on Personality Types

5b. Skills - Listening
Some Skills Used In Having Mindful Listening
A Note on the Use of Meditation

5c. Skills - Feedback
Mindful Visualisation in Feedback
Some Skills Used In Giving Feedback
A Note on Feedback in the Next Session

6. Frameworks For Coaching Sessions
Framework GROW
Extra Framework SMART
Solution Focus Principles, Tools & Frameworks; SIMPLE & OSKAR

Preface

This book is from my perspective. Admittedly a very limited and not very experienced coaching perspective, but perhaps that is an advantage. What I consider to be a definite advantage is the degree in Philosophy, the training as a teacher of religious education, the Masters in theory of contemporary art and performance and the many years working as an artist, sculptor, archaeologist, conservator, dance teacher and writer.

I have completed a course, with practice, in business and executive coaching and found there to be a number of, what I consider to be, obvious theoretical benefits and problems with coaching that didn't seem to be addressed in the literature. So this book is my approach to these issues.

It is my attempt to locate mindfulness within the development of coaching from its origins in sports training in Tim Gallwey's "Inner Game" to its tensions within goal orientated coaching.

The GROWFLOW model contained in this book employs the setting of vertical and horizontal goals and how to combine or to split these kinds of goals in a coaching session. The model can be used as GROW, FLOW or combined as GROWFLOW. It is designed to give insight and knowledge to the novice and expert alike.

We begin with a definition of coaching then look at the pinnacle and balance focussed approaches to goals that coachees and coaches might have. From there we consider the basic elements of coaching of rapport, listening and feedback (with pinnacle focus being more on feedback and balance focus being more on listening and mindfulness). It is then that we look at some traditional coaching frameworks of GROW, SMART and OSKAR. We argue that these are focussed on pinnacle thinking so propose a more balanced, framework of GROWFLOW out of which comes the fully balance based, mindful approach of FLOW. The book ends with a brief discussion of the use of GROWFLOW in creating a coaching culture.

Happy Coaching!

1. Introduction

What is coaching? Coaching is a skill, a life skill that benefits the coach as well as the coachee. The skill is used to create knowledge and perhaps the most important knowledge of a coach is knowledge of themselves. And the from this basis the coach can help their coachees create knowledge by allowing them to come up with their own answers, and directions.

In more detail, coaching is a way to maximise performance and get the most from employees, employers and self. It is a way to improve understanding of ourselves and others and its techniques are simple but effective. There is a process to follow, and a need to be aware of how language can close or open up a conversation. However even silent coaching (where the coach doesn't ask questions) can be effective. Just being committed to the coaching process creates trust and rapport that can transform perspectives on the possibilities for good social and working relations.

Its benefits include more efficiency in work and problem solving, greater job satisfaction, more openness about problems and solutions, and the improving of public relations. This life skill helps the coach find and fulfil their own goals and ambitions as well as those of your coachee.

Definitions of Coaching

A Coach is not a mentor, trainer, consultant, counsellor or therapist. They are more like a Facilitator, Enabler or Developer. There are multiple definitions of these terms and it is not the scope of this essay to provide them all, so we will use some standard definitions for sake of brevity.

A Comparative definition of coaching is given in the Power of Ren;

> "Consultants tend to focus on issues, not on people. A consultant uses information and data to provide professional suggestions and solutions to his client – unlike a coach, who doesn't provide answers. Counsellors and psychiatrists focus on the past, working to resolve old issues and psychological imbalances, whereas a coach focuses on the future, goal-setting, and action. Coaching differs from training also. A trainer provides knowledge and skills to athletes, while a coach helps the client to discover their strengths, identify blind spots, and explore their innate abilities in order to achieve results." 1)

And coaches aren't psychologists because they;
-Focus on helping the coachee with tasks, not solving psychological problems
-Are business like and address real issues
-Moderate the amount and depth of coaching, not overcoach (often coaching in small doses)
-Refer to people with personal problems to a counsellor, not get too involved
-Also keep sight of strategic and operational issues that need decisive action. 2)

So a coach is not a consultant or trainer. They are less concerned with the "nuts and bolts" of developing specific skills and more about the application of skills already learnt (or the way a person learns).

A coach is more like a mentor or supervisor. The term mentor is derived from ancient Greek poetry. Max Landsberg uses a dictionary definition of a mentor to show one to be "a guide, a wise friend and counsellor. In Homer's Odyssey, Mentor was an old friend of Odysseus to whom the latter entrusted his home and his son Telemachus." And Mentor (whose form the Goddess Minerva has assumed) later helps Telemachus find his father. 3)

A coach has similarities to a mentor as both avoid offering advice and let the person follow their own need to learn for themselves. However mentors focus on longer-term, broader issues than a coach and provide key insider information and style changes.

A mentor raises spirits and aspirations and also has a listening ear. And it is worth noting here that a coach is also not a wise, mystic guru or teacher of meditation. These are tempting directions to take for those coaches developing a practice in mindfulness (a technique we will look at later) but they relate more to a spiritual path than to the practical life skill of coaching.

A further useful distinction is between coach (who does the coaching) coachee (who is coached) and client (person for whom the coaching is done) The client might not always be the coachee e.g. it might be the employer who is paying for their manager or worker to be coached.

Additionally the terms coach and coachee can be confusingly similar, yet I think that it is a useful similarity to keep due to the interdependence in the relationship and the closeness with which the two participants are interacting. It also highlights that the concerns of the coachee may be different to those of the client, and there in may lie conflict as the coach's most focussed relationship should be with the coachee. So, at the start of a session, you should set parameters of which goals and feedback are for the client and which for the coachee alone and will be kept private.

All of this is fairly standard to those in the world of coaching but for those outside the term has moved a long way from where most people would originally position it, as connected with athletics and sports coaching. But what are the origins of the term and the limits and boundaries of the term?

Garvey, Stokes and Megginson suggest that the term "coaching" and "coach" comes from sports coaching which in turn comes from a slang term (referred to in Thackeray's 1849 novel *Pendennis*) for an academic tutor who would give university students tuition on a horse-drawn coach down from Oxford. **4)** However, how we understand the term coach is less as a personal academic tutor and more as a rounded aid.

So the cover of this book has a coach journey between two minds or self1 and self2 and these days its not just academic issues but a whole "coach load" of topics.

Driving and Gardening

To get a clearer understanding we need to deconstruct the assumptions behind coaching, so let's play with the term "coach" and this image of a vehicle that it conjures. We want less the idea of you as coach, driving the vehicle, and more the coachee as the person driving. Additionally the vehicle the coachee chooses and the kind of journey they choose to make can be as much a part of their journey as the destination they wish to visit. A Ferrari on a race track or horse and cart down a country lane might reflect the aspirations of a city high flier or a home counties retiree or vice versa.

In our driving metaphor coaches, unlike a driving instructor, don't give the skills to the coachee and, unlike a rally navigator, they don't give the destination and directions to the coachee. The coachee must try to work out how to get to their destination for themselves. In fact they are working out where they actually want to go whilst driving! The coach is more like a "back seat driver". They can offer advice but it won't be well received and so they are better off being like a passenger who is just along for the ride, allowing the driver to explore wherever they like.

This avenue takes us up a bit of a cul-de-sac, so instead lets break down the metaphor further. Our journey is in the mind and the coachee is using the coach's mind as a vehicle. This vehicle is helping them in their travel from one part of their psyche to another. The vehicle must respond to the requirements of the coachee and the coachee needs to learn how to drive the vehicle. Meanwhile the coach must discover where the coachee wants to go and help take them to that place.

This seems counter intuitive as you'd think that the coach is driving the coachee's mind, but that would be more like counselling, therapy or training. Whereas in coaching the coachee is the one facilitated and given the control.

To clarify this metaphor, of the coach's mind as a vehicle for the coachee, perhaps we could look at the 1966 movie "Fantastic Voyage". In which an intrepid team of adventurers is shrunk inside a submarine and sent on a journey into the "inner space" of the body of a nationally important scientist in order to save his life. They travel around the arteries and veins to remove a blood clot to the brain. In our metaphor the coach could be like an "inner space" Brain Pod, that helps the coachee travel from unfulfilled regions of their brain to happy and fulfilled ones. In this way the coach has dual roles of being both a vehicle and the crew in the coachee's inner journey.

However this ridiculous picture of a coach as a vehicle and crew is very mechanistic, technological and science fictional. Our purpose here was to deconstruct the un-thought-through metaphorical term "coach" in order to find it's limitation. A coach as a mere physical vehicle, tool or facility, might transport a person from one place to another but makes no direct change to the inner person during this journey. Instead, we need the coach to be less a "transporter" and more of a "developer" of a person's complex inner potential and "actualiser" of their latent skills and talents.

So a more organic vision of the coach as a gardener may be preferred, growing the client, like a tree or a flower. A life/mind gardener – helping to remove weeds and plant seeds. In this metaphor the first coaching model that we shall look at, GROW, fits very well, and later GROWFLOW, my own model, is perhaps a metaphorical garden with a river or fountain of running water in it - or the national park landscape on the cover of this book through which the coachees travel.

Despite these critical reflections I recognise that "coach" is the established term for a particular activity, and I remain comfortable with the term rather than a term like "developer", "actualiser", "grower" or "gardener". Perhaps this is because not all people want to stay "rooted" to the spot, "growing". Many want to be journeying from one place to another. Having an adventure. The coachee travelling from location to location is mechanistic whilst their developing, like a garden, is organic.

Ultimately the kind of journey or development that a person undertakes will depend upon the kinds of goals that they have. And we will explore these in the next chapter.

2. Goal Setting

The setting of goals is a complex business. The coachee and client will have various issues that they might like to explore. This section is about the principles behind some of these goals and is information for the coach to be aware of but might not be helpful for the coachee to be aware of. In driving it is like the coach being the mechanic (and the coachee being the driver doesn't need to know how the engine and parts work). It might take the coach a number of sessions for the coach to work out where their coachee sits in relation to these general principles.

The goal or journey that the coachee sets themselves or embarks upon can be quite personal or, if they are being coached as part of work, might need to fulfil an employer client's requirements. And what goal your coachee has set will determine how directive you are.

There are many shapes of Goals that a person might set. Whether they have final visions that they aim toward or a belief that we are only ever experiencing in the moment, and that the process and just accepting the "way" that things are is the goal in itself. Does it concerns a journey to a destination or is it the journey along the way that is important. Does the coachee have a specific end or just want to "be".

Goals can be "set in stone" (e.g. win Wimbledon tennis finals) or can be "fluid" (e.g. become as good a player as personally possible). The steps / ways / techniques to reach the goals can be set in stone or fluid. You can even coach with no goals being about the process in general.

Pinnacle goals are usually quite directive and well defined. In contrast, balance goals are more non-directive, allowing a coachee to achieve their own point of balance. An example of this contrast is a person who wants to become a director in a company or partner in a law firm in contrast with a person who is seeking to find the meaning of their life or someone who wants to get a balance between being and doing. They also relate to vehicles and gardening respectively.

Pinnacle & Balance

To make sense of this directly I wish to propose the broad categories of goal of pinnacle or goal of balance.

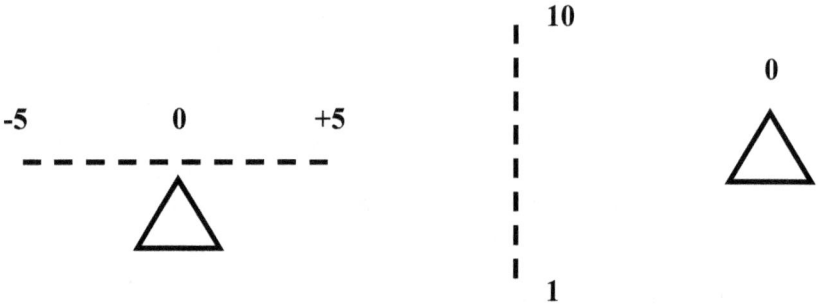

Your goal can be a "Pinnacle" high point "1 to 10" or it can be a process of "Balance" and a mid-point "-5 to +5" or you might ironically have a goal to have no goals, to remove all goals. Setting your Goal at 1-10 is a form of motivation. Setting it at -5 to +5 with 0 at the balance promotes mindfulness and lack of attachment and is more in line with coaching thinking (which we shall look at later).

Pinnacle goals 1to10 seek a vertical progression to a peak end point and have dualistic (e.g. good and bad) value judgments (usually a low value being bad and a high value being good). Balance goals are for a continual process towards an end point beyond values of bad and good, -5to+5. This is neither positive nor negative. It is seeking the mid-point between plus and minus, between good, evil and duality.

Balance is knowing when to allow things to unfold in their own way whereas dualistic thinking of right and wrong, good and evil, causes a split in the mind and creates problems in relationships. In order to bring equilibrium of "being" and "doing" mindfulness can offer a balance to the "doing". You can still be calm whilst "doing". In meditation we can find a still place to "be". There we can "notice" and "let go" – let go so there is no grasping and accept the stream of present moments. 5)

Unfortunately this, the most complex part of the book, comes at the start. However, to try and understand it will bring the reader dividends. mindfulness relates to Buddhist philosophy, which can be very complex. I hope to present the concepts here in an accessible way.

A scale of -5to+5 helps represent the Buddhist view that the world is suffering and that suffering is the result of "attachment" to both positive and negative desires and experiences and that the only release from this is in the absolute balance that is Nirvana, Enlightenment.

At this point we need to make a distinction between a pinnacle balance and a true balance. A work / life balance scale is like having two pinnacles that you might wish to reach. Both work and life can have positive ratings. The coachee may be happy to have different ratings for the different areas of their lives and the balance issue becomes how far can they go out on these scales, before they become overstretched e.g. +2, +3? They also might have three, four, five or more pinnacle arrows leading off into different goals, like spokes of a wheel, and as such it is less a balancing scale and more a collection of goals that need managing.

A truer balance has a single factor that has a positive and negative direction, such as "sensation" which in a positive sense is pleasure and in a negative sense is pain. The question here is how far out on this scale can you go before becoming "attached" to the single factor. On this true balance scale the balance is about having equal weight at equal points, or the weight dead centre. To remove attachment the goal is to be in the middle - as if you are attached to either pain (or rather its avoidance) or pleasure you will have an unbalance that gives suffering. If you are attached at -2 and +2 then you might be squeamish or a hedonist in equal measure, however, your real goal is to bring your weights together, to unite them in your true inner self, and to maintain a balance. This can be done most easily by uniting them all at point 0.

So pinnacle balance is about multiple counters progressing up multiple scales whereas a true (mindful) balance is about uniting the counters at point 0. A pinnacle balance e.g. +2 work and +2 life positions, might give an intimation of the true balance, resembling the experience of being at point 0, but it is different to the inner journey of true balance through non-attachment.

However, if you have a balance goal that doesn't mean that you don't have specific targets it is just that the process is more important.

"Confucius says ... if you shoot for the stars and hit the moon, it's OK. But you've got to shoot for something. A lot of people don't even shoot." **6)** If you don't aim for a target you won't hit the target – it is just your attachment to hitting or missing the target that is the problem as this can cause interference. We could describe this position as balance or pinnacle where you might be +10 on a scale it is just that the balanced person doesn't strive to be higher up the scale or fear being lower on it, just allow themselves to remain balanced where they are.

With having ambitious positive goals there is also a creative striving to overcome the status quo and unsettle balance. Henry Ford said that "if I had listened to what my customers believed they wanted...I would've made a faster horse!" **7)**

Mindfulness, Self1, Self2 & Self3

The contrast between the two approaches is highlighted by the ideas of coaching for compassion and for compliance. Liz Hall describes how Richard Boyatzis "Coaching For Compassion" (which I suggest is balance based) is helping people be who they should be, rather than an ideal self. This is opposed to "Coaching for Compliance" (pinnacle based) which is about trying to fix problems rather than just allowing situations to be. **8)**

The first is compassionate is because if people are not reaching their pinnacle goals then discrepancy scaling stress can arise. If we don't focus on winning then, suggests Liz Hall, we can avoid discrepancy based processing – e.g. if we set too high a goal to not have bad feelings then it can lead to us being more depressed if we can't control having the bad feelings in the first place. Hall describes how mindfulness, can help us evaluate, gain perspective and see our negative evaluations as temporary rather than fixed. **9)**

This mindfulness also helps us deal with uncertainty, not-knowing and not being perfect. It helps us to stay flexible and steer away from "what if" scenarios. **10)** Being Mindful we are neither positive or negative, we are just in the moment. We can then choose the positive and also have the benefits of control.
11)

This talk of mindfulness and meditation might seem to the reader way off the mark (depending on the goal they have in reading this book). However, the key to effective coaching is to be able to recognise and distinguish pinnacle and balance mindsets in coachees. Furthermore, mindfulness links back to the original philosophy of coaching by Gallwey in the Inner Game.

> "By ending judgment, you do not avoid seeing what is. Ending judgment means that you neither add nor subtract from the fact before your eyes. Things appear as they are – undistorted. In this way, the mind becomes more calm." **12)**

This means that you don't distort what you see and so can see what is really there. And for Gallwey we have two main selves; self1 = ego mind (self-conscious thinking and feeling) and self2 = body / mind (the intuitive being and reactions in a person). When self1 is not judgmental of self2 then trust and self confidence develop and effective action results. **13)**

Disturbance often comes because we are attached to thinking and situations so we can remove that disturbance by letting go of attachments. A Zen Master said the most important work in English is "let", "let it be," "let it happen." Let go and allow the joy to come into your life (or problems to be solved in the unconscious mind) instead of contriving to have a good time. **14)**

There is a huge assumption here, that, as humans, our natural state is to be in balance and that our seeking to be extreme in any sphere is unnatural. Rather it is emotional attachment to the success or failure of an endeavour which is the cause of unbalance. We may have an "unbalanced" endeavour of "shooting for the stars" and still be balanced about our attachment to success or failure in this endeavour – although the higher the goal the harder it is to remain balanced. Thus our natural dispositions, talents and goals can differ from person to person but we can all seek a balance in how attached we are to our goals. Gallwey rejects the attachment to pinnacle goals for their own sake.

> "speaking as a man who once was a compulsive self-improver, I want to make it clear that the last thing I wish to do is to encourage any notion that you should be any different from what you are right now. I say this with great conviction because I spent many not-so-happy years trying to become "better" than I thought I was, trying to change into somebody I thought I should be. And I lost touch with who and what I truly was act on?" **15)**

This focus is on a balance scale rather than a pinnacle scale and although an archer may aim to hit the centre of a target their balance is in not being "attached" to hitting the target. We will look at this technique later as our concern at the moment is for our general approach to goal setting rather than the specific achievement of goals.

The balance is not about content, e.g. balance of work and life, but about the approach of attachment, e.g. about not being attached to being either a good or a bad coach, just using skill in being a coach. It is not about will but about skill. A person could be completely balanced (in terms of not being attached to good or bad results) even if they are completely focussed on work, whereas someone else with work / life more in balance might run around frantically trying to get things achieved and be ineffective due to being too attached to the success of the ventures.

However, the pinnacle goals are traditionally seen as work goals and the balance goals as lifestyle goals. This gives the interesting conundrum of whether you put work / life combinations into a balance scale or into a pinnacle scale.

I introduced the -5to+5 balance scaling when looking at Work / Life balance for one of my coachee's, asking them to place themselves on where they thought they were in that balance of work or leisure. I used scaling to work out the work life balance with a tipping scale of work one side and life the other side. I felt that the coachee was already overworked, working from 9am -9pm yet she wanted to work more and felt that she was having too much leisure. There was no point in challenging this as the coachee was entrenched at that moment. And it showed that a balance scale was also on a Pinnacle scale.

I've since found a Work / Life balance is too clumsy for measuring attitudes to work and life as both work and leisure can be positive so a balance of plus and minus doesn't reflect this. You need a Work / Leisure / Pleasure / Displeasure Matrix as you might have an excess of Work yet enjoy this, or an excess of Leisure and find this unrewarding and un-enjoyable.

In conversation with Stephanie Sturges about my relating pinnacle and balance scaling she originated the idea of the "Sturges Triangle". This grows along the horizontal or vertical depending on how focussed on the pinnacle or balance goals a person is.

The Sturges Triangle

a) balance and pinnacle

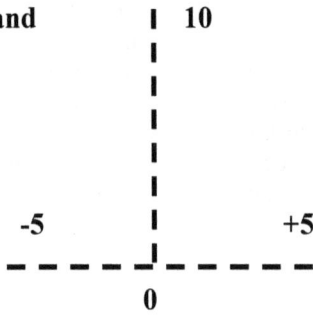

```
                    I   10
                    I
                    I
                    I
                    I
     -5             I            +5
     — — — — —I— — — — —
                    0
```

b) mainly balance

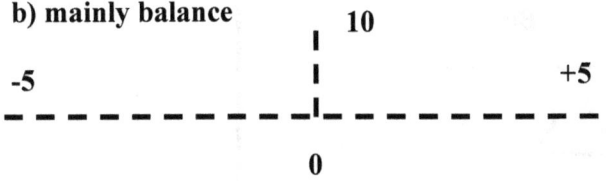

```
                        I   10
-5                      I                    +5
— — — — — — — — —I— — — — — — — —
                        0
```

c) mainly pinnacle

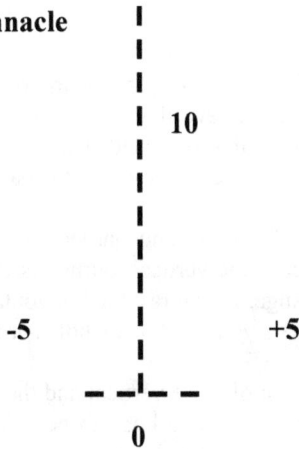

```
                    I
                    I
                    I   10
                    I
                    I
                    I
                    I
     -5             I       +5
                    I
                    I
          — —I— —
                    0
```

I have translated this into a system of dashes, the total quantity of which remains the same, to illustrate how people have hardwired into their thought systems the two different ways of thinking. It is interesting to note that on this model the pinnacle scale starts at 0, showing the interconnection between the two scalings. This explains how, even if they focus on one way of looking, they can still consider that they do both ways of thinking. A pinnacle person will be competitive in their balance thinking and a balance person will be less ambitious in their pinnacle thinking. This can result in a situation where c) imposes their pinnacle value system on b) who values balance and yet c) still believes that they consider balance fairly. Another way to look at this is:

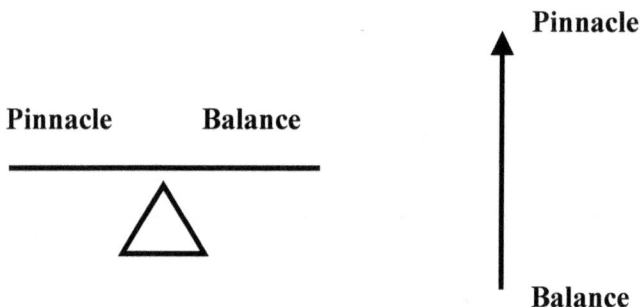

Pinnacle

Pinnacle   **Balance**

Balance

In this model a) the balance thinkers try to incorporate pinnacle thinking but b) the pinnacle thinkers believe that they supersede balance. Again this analysis is key, as depending on whether a person is in pinnacle or balance orientation will determine the best way to coach that person.

Extending the metaphor of driving and gardening to the pinnacle and balance scaling we can see if the vertical journey is flying in a plane, or climbing up a mountain range. In contrast the horizontal line of GROW is not just a tree, which marks a vertical, but a whole garden spread out.

People are actually a mixture of these vertical and the horizontal goals of doing and being. All that we want to hope to be able to establish, over time, the general mode in which a coachee wants to do or be.

At the end of the Inner Game we learn of Gallwey's ultimate goal. This is to find self3 who aims at true balance on the scale. This prime goal of the

Inner Game is direct experience of the origin of every experience. Self3 is consciousness aware of itself. It can be experienced by any human being when his desire for it is sufficiently sincere. It is direct experience of a human's full potential and unfolds without interference from self1. The person is then free and can express with love his unique humanness, talents and circumstances. **16)**

However, whilst this might be the goal of the Inner Game this mystical extreme is just one of a myriad of options that a coach might help unfold for the coachee.

The kind of coaching that a person gets should depend on the kinds of goals and approaches that they have. T. Gallwey created a psychological model that can be used to help coachees achieve their Skills by removing interference. It is driving without worry about how to drive, or not allowing distractions to interfere with the driving. And in gardening it is getting on with the job of allowing unimpeded growth.

Whilst Gallwey posits three selves it is the first two that concern most interaction. He posits that each person has an internal teller (self 1) and doer (self 2) and better action (e.g. tennis) is produced through improving the relationship between self 1 and self 2. When the teller interferes too much with the doer then it inhibits the action. The way to stop trying too hard and to use effort and energy effectively is to i) program self 2 with images not words, ii) trust self 2 can do what self 1 asks, iii) see non-judgmentally i.e. see what happens without "good" or "bad" valuing. Gallwey refers to the archery of D.T. Suzuki the Zen master. Don't deliberate and conceptualise. Let the 2 selves unite. When self1 isn't criticising then Effortless action flows. "During such experiences, the mind does not act like a separate entity telling you what you should do or criticising how you do it. It is quiet, you are "together" and the action flows as free as a river." It is concentrating without "trying" to concentrate. **17)**

The way to achieve a still mind is to just stop thinking. It is hard and requires letting go of habits learnt as a child. Letting go of judging ourselves and performances as good or bad. "When we unlearn how to be judgmental it is possible to achieve spontaneous, concentrated play." This is to employ the coaching skill of mindfulness which we shall look at in more detail later. The idea is to not make value judgment and to just receive objective information, e.g. an umpire judging with detached interest as opposed to players who feel some shot is good or bad, positive or negative, like or disliked. The act of judging begins the evaluative, thinking process and so creates distraction. The mind judges particulars, then generalises and creates rules judging against itself and impeded performance becomes a self fulfilling prophecy. This is not to ignore that you might be playing into the net. It is to stop yourself labelling it as "bad" which creates a reaction. And it is best to use non-descriptive words as this helps keep the player relaxed and fluid. **18)**

In tennis it is not observing what is right and wrong, just feeling / knowing where the racquet is in a given situation. Eventually your use of it will naturally improve. Self2 is seen as a fantastically sophisticated processor of information. Mistrust of self2 lead to trying too hard (to using too many muscles) and too much self instruction (too much mental distraction). Trusting self2 is not positive thinking (e.g. believing that you will hit the ball), instead it is just letting yourself hit the ball. The idea is not to identify with the backhand or the forehand hit as if it is not working you may become personally upset. Just "let it happen" and if it doesn't then know how to do this then "let it learn." And here we assume the skill and technique has already been taught. Then learn by practice as this refines the action. However, self1 can also help by setting goals, i.e. by letting self2 know what it wants to do and then trusting self2 to do it. **19)**

It is interesting that Gallwey also uses a gardening metaphor, pointing out that we don't criticise the seed of a rose for not having roots. It shoots out of the earth and develops over time. It is not criticised for having roots or flowers when not at the right stage of development. The same with our own progress. Don't criticise it inappropriately. Don't identify with them as they are just stages. And when you remove "judgment" you can see things as they are. **20)**

When self1 controls actions the ego gets a sense of achievement. When self2 is in control then it isn't ego in control and the satisfaction is elsewhere. If self1 takes credit because it did the relaxing then it will try and control the relaxing and inhibit self2 in fully relaxing. "Relaxing" is allowed and is not the result of "trying" or "making". **21)**

Gallwey argues that the development of peoples' abilities can be impaired by over-analysing a situation and being too attached to the results of their actions. That a natural development can occur (that is the refinement of Skills) if the interference is removed by staying in self2. Self1 takes all credit for reaching goals – good and bad – which makes it liable to make judgmental interferences whereas self2 is more effective and just lets things happen and remains humble.

From all this it might seem like Gallwey wants to reject self1, however he sees self1 as contributing to the development of the person allowing self2 to come out by the ideals that self1 sets. Eventually if self2 is allowed to fully develop then self3 can emerge. In effect self2 only exists in a relationship to self1. When that relationship goes then self3 can emerge. However, too much control by self1 prevents even self2 from appearing.

"in the language of karma yoga, this is called action without attachment to the fruits of action, and ironically when the state is achieved the results are the best possible." Karma Yoga is a Hindu mystical practice. That his philosophy reflects this perspective is reinforced by Gallwey. 22) "as an instructor of yoga tennis, I didn't concern myself with winning; I simply attempted to achieve and express a high degree of excellence." 23)

When a player sees concentration and the Inner Game is more important than the Outer Game of Tennis then they can play best. And as both games occur at the same time it is a matter of which deserves priority. Let go of judging and welcome obstacles as a way to increase abilities and find advantage. 24)

In criticism of this Wong and Leung in "Power of Ren" say that T. Gallwey Inner Game is seen as Zen-like but real Zen is about meditation so the average Chinese person wouldn't link Zen meditation and tennis. Rather, the Inner Game is more about unlocking potential. 25)

Wong and Leung argue that the Chinese are influenced by Confucianism, Buddhism and Taoism. They argue that these philosophies seek to harmonise the inner and outer selves. However, they argue, Confucius looked to the person, not the issue, first. 26) "Ren" means people so Ren coaching is about people and not issues or practical skills 27). So this is slightly different in focus from improving "doing" to improving "being" and Wong and Leung even claims coaching should aim at a broader social role. People should study, observe and think deeply, then lead by example.

They continue that Confucian philosophy underpins 20 centuries of Chinese thought. Its 2 main strands are; harmonise your inner nature with your outer nature, and, from top to bottom of society cultivation of the person is the root of everything else. Ren coaching focuses on this with the 2 strokes of the character being "Aspects". Ren has an Inner (potential) self and an Outer (externally expressed) self gained over the years (knowledge and skills). Laozi said "In pursuit of knowledge, we gain day by day." But added. "In the pursuit of the way (dao), we discard day by day." This is knowing what "knowledge" interferes with actual doing and not allowing it. Simultaneous gaining and losing is the essence of the Ren Coaching Model. **28)**

In the Two Aspects - the inner self needs to put to good use the knowledge gained from the outer self and get rid of what isn't needed. The inner self has to grow along with the skills that the outer self is acquiring. Martial Arts Swordsmen need to be one with their sword to be two perfectly matched objects. **29)** This seems aligned to the Inner Game of Tennis developing the Skills rather than the criticism they make its not developing the person **30)** and the tennis is just one skill of many whether personal or practical.

However, what both Gallwey and Wong and Leung in "Power of Ren" might agree upon is the formula (P=p-i) performance is potential minus interference. Coaching removes interference by creating cooperation and removing complaining by self1. **31)**

3. Does Coaching Develop Will or Skill?

The previous discussion has been about general goals and it is useful to find where, in relation to their goal, the coachee sits in terms of the Will/Skill Matrix, as this displays what direction the coach might want to travel with the coachee. This is particularly useful if a specific goal has been required by the client. Again, this is not something that is explicitly discussed with the coachee. Rather it is skilfully discovered by the coach in the course of discussion with the coachee (and possibly with the client beforehand).

There are four main combinations according to the Will/Skill Matrix. In driving I think this is like a company director who wants their drivers coaching. His four types of worker are the over-cautious learner driver who must develop the skill and is not really interested to learn, the over-confident learner driver who keenly races around but doesn't have the skills, the advanced driver who loves to drive and drives well, and the experienced driver who has many skills but is now nervous and reticent on the road.

Guide (high will Low skill)	Delegate (high will High skill)
Direct (low will Low skill)	Excite (low will High skill

Skill is experience, training, understanding, role perception. Will is desire to achieve, incentives, security, confidence. The combinations of low and high skill and will produce 4 quadrants on the matrix. Each quadrant has an appropriate management style for an employee with the aim being to move the employee from low to high in the areas. **32)**

Low will and low skill – Direct. Give clear briefing and motivate with easily attainable skill training targets. Give feedback and praise. Supervise closely with clear rules and deadlines.

Low will and high skill – Excite. Find reasons for low will, e.g. if there are task / management style or personal factors. Then motivate and monitor feedback.

High will and low skill – Guide. Invest time to train in skills in a risk free environment with a relaxed control.

High will and high skill – Delegate. Give freedom to do the job in their own way and give praise. Involve them in responsible decision making and get their opinion. Give stretching tasks and don't over-manage them.

If there is high will present then coaching can be used most effectively for maintaining motivation to pinnacle goals or helping achieve balance through mindfulness. However, it is most effective when there is a will deficit as the coach can offer structure and directives/direction in the form of prompts and encouragements. This is where coaching can be used most effectively for motivating towards pinnacle goals or moving forward in mindfulness.

When there are problems with a skill or will deficit then, tor me, this model needs an extra layer which coaching can uncover e.g. learning to drive where if you don't have the "skill to drive" or the "will to drive". Then you need the "will to learn to drive" and the "skill to learn to drive" e.g. the ability to learn i.e. sense of responsibility, hand to foot coordination, manual dexterity. And if you don't have these then you need the more general "will to learn" and the "skill to learn" i.e. ability to read and concentrate. One of my coachees, a student, wanted to work harder but didn't find work motivating. Eventually her friends helped her by working / studying together with her. This gave her the will to learn.

As an aside – I think that "Will" should not be confused with motivation as you can be motivated to act but not willing to act e.g. to drive, until you have properly learned what to do. Motivation is general and willingness is specific. Without the skill in knowing how to be motivated and enthused then the willingness to do tasks can fade and this can lead to burn out etc. in more convoluted terms this might be seen as the will or skill that is needed to have will or skill.

Returning to the Will/Skill Matrix, I relate will to pinnacle self1 and skill to balance self2. In this sense the pinnacle coaching can help develop the coachee's will or balance coaching can help to remove it, to allow the coachee to just act skilfully and "effectively".

Coach, Coachee, Will & Skill

It can also be useful to note that, just like the coachee, the coach has their own Will/Skill Matrix that they need to be aware of. Determining where someone is in terms of Will/Skill depends on what goal has been set. But if the goal is not clear then the coach needs skill to get the coachee there. So the coachee's will may be to find a goal and here the coach's skill can help. A coach with low skill and high will doesn't understand the limits of coaching and might over-promise on what they can deliver. You mustn't confuse the Will/Skill of the coachee e.g. the tennis player, with the Will/Skill of the coach. Coaching is a balance between Will/Skill of the coach and the coachee.

The following table shows both the influence of the Will/Skill of the coach on the coachee and can also be used to show the influence of the coachee's own will / skill at mindfulness upon themselves.

As mentioned, there are similarities between self1 to will and self2 to skill on the Will/Skill Matrix. This assumes that the person has skill in themselves already and they need to stop their will from interfering with that skill. This requires a skill of mindfulness and the will to use a mindful approach.

1. Guide The Task (high will / low skill)		4. Delegate The Task (high will / high skill)	
Seek Mindfulness (high will? low skill)	Perfect Mindfulness (no will? high skill)	Seek Mindfulness (high will? low skill)	Perfect Mindfulness (no will? high skill)
Try Mindfulness (low will? low skill)	Develop Mindfulness (low will? high skill	Try Mindfulness (low will? low skill)	Develop Mindfulness (low will? high skill
2. Direct The Task (low will / low skill)		3. Excite The Task (low will / high skill)	
Seek Mindfulness (high will? low skill)	Perfect Mindfulness (no will? high skill)	Seek Mindfulness (high will? low skill)	Perfect Mindfulness (no will? high skill)
Try Mindfulness (low will? low skill)	Develop Mindfulness (low will? high skill	Try Mindfulness (low will? low skill)	Develop Mindfulness (low will? high skill

A Will/Skill Matrix of mindfulness is inserted in each quadrant. Again the low will / high skill quadrant might be more receptive than high will and high skill to the use of mindfulness as it produces less interference for the coachee, e.g. a tennis player with a high will to perform might not want to follow a coaching process whereas one with a lower will might recognise its value in being able to increase skill without interference from will. However, coaching can be used to help develop the will to act and learn and also allow skills to function or help the coachee learn new skills by removing the interference of will from performance.

On a deeper level it might be argued that mindfulness is actually all Skill as it involves the removal of all Will. This is borne out by mindfulness being a skill that takes years of practice to develop and has to be regularly practiced or it is lost. This implies that the true progression of mindfulness is not from low will / high skill towards high will / high skill but rather it is towards No will / high skill, which may form part of a definition of self3. The greater the mindfulness skill the less the will. However, this discussion is metaphysical and, along with descriptions of self3, are outside the scope of this book.

Many clients might want their coachee to develop a higher will in the workplace, even though the coach can recognise that this might interfere with their use of skill in self2. And we shall later see how the use of Feedback can help in achieving such pinnacle goals.

Resistance To Coaching

As well as Will / Skill in relation to the coachee's task and the coach's abilities there is also Will / Skill in relation to the coachee's willingness to undertake coaching. The coach may encounter resistance to coaching, and experience the limits of what coaching can do and how far people are prepared to change or actually can change. Resistance to coaching can be seen as having Low Will to undertake the coaching process. And this is linked to resistance to change which has been described in the change curve devised by Elizabeth Kulber Ross and in the 4-room Apartment designed by Claes Janssen. **33)**

4 – Room Apartment

Contentment	Renewal
Denial	Confusion

It works anti-clockwise and describes the stages that we go through when confronted by change.

Denial – and hoping that the unwanted situation will go away.

Confusion – anger, resentment and blame at self and others.

Renewal – testing the new situation and finding advantages.

Contentment – integrating into a new whole or accepting the inevitability of the change.

Coaching can help people be more open to change, feel listened to in change and be less defensive when problems arise. However, coaching cannot change people who do not want to engage with the coaching process. People who do not want coaching in an organisation may be hard to convince. I think that this can be plotted onto the Will Skill Matrix (with the matrix rotated 90 degrees anti-clockwise to fit onto the 4-room apartment).

Contentment	Renewal
High Will	*Low Will*
High Skill	*High Skill*
Denial	Confusion
High Will	*Low Will*
Low Skill	*Low Skill*

In general the reluctance is from will as the coachee might see coaching as an exercise of will (and possibly manipulative) rather than understand it as a use of skills. This lack of understanding of the coaching process and skill set is due to lack of knowledge / information. This can be in addition to the resistance to whatever issue it is that the coaching is also needed for.

To overcome reluctance to being coached you should consider the various aspects of the relationship before offering coaching. If there is mistrust of you or the organisation then build trust between you. If the organisation or yourself are seen as judgmental then explain what your role in the organisation is and that coaching is non evaluative. Coaching needs to be informal/confidential, not on company personnel files.

The coachee might be untrusting of the process or you as a person or coach. If you have a different style to the coachee then explain the different styles. The coachee might also need control over the process – a way to help this might be to agree specific times to coach. Also if the coachee won't respond to your approach – ask how the coachee would like the feedback/coaching. Finally, the coachee might also not believe that they need to change, so, get facts to show it is needed. And if they don't need it then reassess your leadership skills. **34)**

Sometimes we can be confused into thinking that a person (or an organisation) is not an "agent for change" when really it is due to the coach not allowing the coaching process to unfold. The best way to bring about non-forced change is to give the coachees space so that they can come up with the solutions themselves.

"The secret for the coach is to create a compelling vision for people to buy into." To create a picture in the coachee's mind, asking "What will success look like, what will you see happening, hear yourself saying, feel?" "How does this inspire you?" **35)**

This process can also happen for organisations and the leader, as coach, is the person who can embed coaching in the culture of the organisation by good example and inspirational vision. And as a coachee I like to get an overview of issues and feel a bit rushed into actions if I don't explore the issues that I want to. This doesn't mean that I'm not an agent for change, I just want to explore and change my views before setting my actions. I need the coach to steer to the issue I want to look at and to be attentive to my issues.

4. A Coach Focusses, Expands and Delves Deep

Model T + Interference (Skill)

We've looked at the need for removing the interference of will on the development of skill but with coaching you're not just exercising this skill. You are usually finding and exploring around a coachee's will and what their goals are. These are usually set by a person's self1.

Model T is a model that combines the removal of interference with a wilful focus on what the coachee wants. By focussing on a topic/goal for discussion you then remove general interference of self1. However, by expanding on the topic you bring out the other issues involved. The horizontal bar of the "T" is to "expand" and the vertical is to "focus" down. This is to summarise and then expand the number of options but stay focussed on the topic and issues. This removes interference and allows the full use of skill by the coach and the coachee. **36)**

After the coachee's expanding of the topic the coach helps the coachee focus on what is interesting. The coach's use of summary, i.e. summarising the points made by the coachee, helps the coachee stay focussed. (Model T) is where expanding interest drives focus which in turn removes interference. **37)**

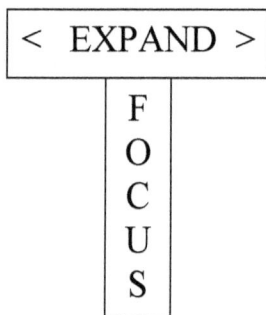

```
┌─────────────────────┐
│  <   EXPAND   >     │
└─────────┬───────────┘
        │ F │
        │ O │
        │ C │
        │ U │
        │ S │
        └───┘
```

This is the smallest structure for coaching but does not bring in the full range of skills of a coach. More complex structures, frameworks like GROW will be considered later.

It should be noted that the coach can also benefit from the use of Model T. As the coach must focus on the coachee and help expand their issues.

Taking our driving metaphor you could almost look on it as a Ford Model T (the first mass produced car and the basis of the factory production in modern motoring). It is driving surrounded by noise and distractions so the driver must focus but also needs to be aware of where they are going. In gardening it is focussing on a particular flowerbed when the garden is full of weeds and distractions, but remaining aware of other needs in the garden.

Deeper Levels (Will)

Expanding and deepening your areas of focus can bring scrutiny to bear upon a number of areas of will and self1 that might be unexpected.

All your previous attributes – purposes, identity, beliefs, values and capabilities show themselves in everything that you do in your behaviour. This behaviour is the tip of the "Iceberg", the bit that you say and what you do that is the visible part of your attributes. Companies can also have behaviours characteristic of them as a company or in various departments and teams. Plans can be set for changing behaviours and we should focus on the patterns of behaviour and not on the content if we want to make a change. **38)**

This model of the "Iceberg" shows that there is much that lies beneath the surface of a coachee. However, as a metaphor it is limited as it doesn't allow what's below the surface to come above the surface. For this I propose the "Volcano", which is largely dormant but can bring issues from the inner self out to the surface, often with explosive effect. And this then forms the new surface.

ICEBERG   VOLCANO

Behaviour

Above the surface   What you say and what you do   Behaviour

Purpose, identity, beliefs, values and capabilities

Below the surface

Purpose, identity, beliefs, values and capabilities

Unconscious

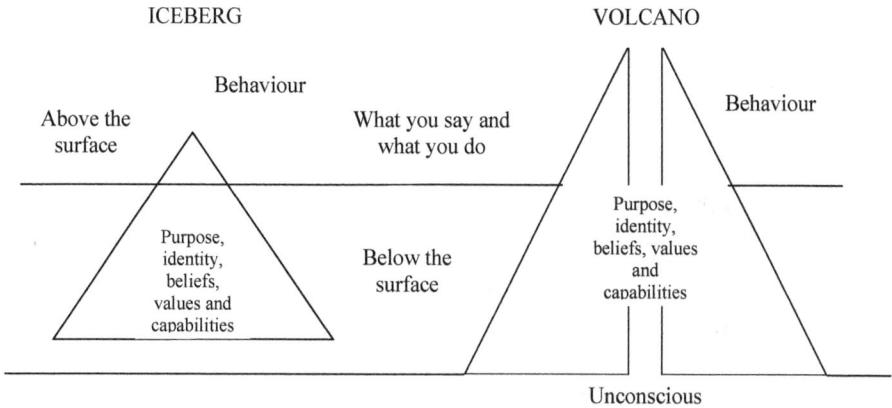

Expanding and deepening focus to look at deeper issues can be productive in raising some of these issues to the surface but, because you are operating from a deeper place, it can also raise issues that are not relevant to the topic, e.g. one of my coachees had a volcanic emotional overflow (burst into tears) when asked about not being valued at work. I valued her in this expression. It was produced by pointing out an issue in their volcano and was then allowed appropriate expression. At a later date I had a volcano issue pointed out that wasn't conducive to the coaching session. I felt like I was taken to a deeper emotional place that was a side issue. So when another of my coachees had a deeper issue of inter-colleague valuing that arose, like a volcano, I didn't pursue it because I felt that it was the wrong track to take.

In order to avoid raising non-relevant emotional issues it is important to keep the goal of the coachee in mind and to follow a defined framework, which also allows a person to get to the deeper issues in a more managed way. We shall come to these after looking at some of the skills needed in coaching.

In driving, the driving is in difficult terrain and the more that you explore a region the more likely you are to find yourself in potentially dangerous ground. And in gardening you are never quite sure what you might dig up.

5. Skills For Coaching Sessions

General Coach's Skills

We've looked at the general approaches to coaching and understanding different kinds of goals, now lets look at more specific techniques for coaching.

In coaching we need to develop three aspects of Skills e.g. listening, Frameworks e.g. GROW and Principles e.g. SIMPLE. The skills are the qualities that can be involved in coaching even without a framework. The framework helps give direction and form to make the skills even more effective. And the principles help to finesse the procedure.

> "Coaching aims to enhance the performance and learning ability of others. It involves providing feedback, but it also uses other techniques such as motivation, effective questioning and consciously matching your management style to each coachee's readiness to undertake a particular task." **39)**

This is an example of a quote from one of many books on coaching with a different list of qualities, skills and tools for coaches. The skills listed often overlap. Asking what skills make a good coach is like asking in driving – what makes a good vehicle and driving companion? Or in gardening – what makes a good gardener? It is all relative to the coachee. However, it will be illuminating to give structure to these skills so I have put them into a simple order of beginnings, middle and endings of a coaching session. This is a minimal directive structure for a coaching session and corresponds loosely with Rapport, Listening and Feedback.

This follows the communication cycle: initiation, response, acknowledgment **40)** and gives the basic idea that you begin by establishing Rapport at the start of the session. Then you progress the coachee's toward their goals by being attentive with mindful listening toward them. The coachee is allowed to speak or express themselves and are only questioned when they don't have anything else to say or are straying from the issue .Finally you give the coachee Feedback that makes their issues more concrete. However, you return to your core skills and interweave them throughout the coaching process.

The placing of these skills into these categories is open to debate and many terms fall between the categories. However, what is notable is that the most numerous skills are involved in Feedback, however, it is

Rapport and Listening mindfully that are the more effective skills in non-directive coaching, whilst Feedback is more key to directive coaching.

Directive vs Non – Directive Principles

So far our metaphor of coaching puts the coachee in the driving and navigational seats. This is non-directive coaching but the coach isn't completely non-directive and fluid. They are there to help the coachee with some directive structure if they need it.

In the driving metaphor, instead of being like an understanding travel companion who is happy to go along for the ride, if they have been commissioned by the client then they have a destination to help the driver reach. They don't have the freedom to have no goal and just allow the person space to find their goal. The non-directive coach can be like a pillion passenger on a motorcycle – like "Easy Rider", just travelling, ready to talk with the driver but putting no pressure on them. Instead the directive coach needs to offer more advice and guidance on routes. In between the two is the gardener who plants the right seeds that the client wants to see and then allows them to grow. Watering and nurturing at the appropriate moments. Giving their expertise as to what is possible - but all to the clients vision.

There are 4 levels of non-directive & directive: 1. non-directive free thinking, 2. a coaching framework (like GROW which we shall describe later), 3. directive, exercises, 4. fully directive advice, instruction and training. What dictates their use is whether it raises awareness and leaves responsibility with the client, with level 4 as the least effective and only of use when the other levels are effective. **41)**

In a non-directive approach there is no requirement of results from the coachee, whereas the more directive, approach is goal orientated and requires giving feedback on progress. You need to tailor your approach to the individual needs of the client / coachee. Providing non-directive coaching for a client who is just interested in exploring possibilities is appropriate whereas providing it for a client who wants to set themselves some specific steps towards a greater goal is misguided.

Whilst there appears to be an inherent contradiction in using coaching as a non-directive tool for setting directive goals the coach is providing for the different facets of a client (directive or non-directive) at any particular moment and needs to be flexible.

This tension in the uses of coaching is partly due to its being inherently non-directive and balance focussed but it has been increasingly used in business for directive, pinnacle ends. A directive manager using directive ends would instruct and tell their worker what to do. The difference between mindfulness and coaching given by Liz Hall (in the table below) also characterises the difference between directive and non-directive principles. With someone who is pinnacle focussed not necessarily being more receptive to directive coaching, just more used to that kind of approach.

Table of the areas of difference between Mindfulness and Coaching. **42)**

Mindfulness	Coaching
Attending to the present moment	Future – focussed
Non-striving / letting go	Striving
Non-goal orientated	Goal - focussed
Being	Doing
Accepting what is	Trying to change what is
Non-attachment	Attachment e.g. to goal
Lots of silence	Lots of words
Solitary (not always)	Involves two or more people (apart from self-coaching)
Sense of one-ness	Often focussed on individual's agenda (but should consider system)

A person might wish to be pinnacle or balance in their goals and how they get there can be directive or non-directive. Someone who wants their life focus to change from balance scaling might need directive coaching at first and later a non-directive approach or they might need to begin from a non-directive approach.

The key thing is not to impose your ideas upon the coachee but to identify if they want to be listened to (and just need to talk and express their thoughts) or whether they are at an impasse (and would like to receive direction through some kind of questioning).

All questioning involves some kind of direction in the coaching. So a non-directive approach will have less questioning, just mindful listening, until the end of the session when the questioning will just be for finding a way forward. Consequently Non-directive coaching involves a focus on Rapport and Listening mindfully whereas directive coaching involves more of a focus on Feedback. A non-directive approach follows: Rapport, Mindfulness (with Model T to Focus) and Feedback. A directive approach follows: Rapport, Mindfulness, Questions (with Model T to Expand), Visualisations for the Ways Forward and Feedback.

Again, non-directive is like sitting in the car and listening to the driver (coachee) whereas directive is clarifying routes and suggesting short-cuts and places to stop etc.

Summary Of A Skills Based Coaching Session

1a. Set the context
- build trust and rapport
- if first time then explain what coaching is, if a repeat sessions then review the previous sessions achievable steps
- establish the client's and the coachee's Goals
- diagnose the Will and Skill of the coachee for the task

1b. The next part of this stage requires great skill on the coach's part. It is not necessary before coaching can begin and may need discovering over a number of sessions. Addressing it directly is not advised as it may confuse the coachee and undermine rapport;
- determine whether the Goals are pinnacle or balance focussed,
- discover how the coach and coachee's selves (1 or 2) might interact,
- agree the approach e.g. non-directive mindfulness or directive feedback

2. Provide coaching
- use structured sessions with mindful listening and / or feedback to help create achievable steps towards goals as required (30-60 minutes)

3. Conclude effectively
- encourage coachee to reflect on what's learned over the sessions

5a. Skills - Rapport

Rapport with a coachee is essential in forming a relationship that is likely to facilitate addressing issues. And generally speaking, if you are open about the coaching process, sincere and compassionate in your approach then you will generate the rapport required to get your coachee into a trusting focus. This is enhanced by mirroring your coachee's language (both verbal and physical / bodily).

The creation of rapport begins before the start of your coaching session. It is in the set-up to the session as well.

To set up your first coaching sessions you can send information to the coachee about the principles of the coaching process to explain what coaching is. You can give them some forms to fill out briefly before the session to help them focus their minds. The initial eliciting of a person's values is important as it will also help the coach get direction.

A pre-coaching questionnaire could be used and / or a wheel of life and/or a wheel of work, where each segment of a circle represents an area of interest and you shade in how full you are in that segment. Wheel of Life – e.g. partner, work, money, health, friends, environment, personal development, fun. Wheel of Work – e.g. leadership, problem solving, planning and budgeting, teamwork, delegation, communication, managing change, time management. **43)** Alternatively you might use a "Star-Ball" of pinnacle spokes which the coachee rates from 1-10.

Using the wheel helps establish the coachee's areas of surplus and deficit and primary focus for the session. They can also be used to establish interests if there is an impasse on "Ways Forward" in a session. This is a more positive route than seeing a Coachee as not being a "customer for change". Filling these out at different stages of the coaching can show how the coachee is progressing and are a way to help the coachee keep faith that the coaching process, will bring about options in time.

In addition to the wheel or star-ball you can also give the coachees a balance and ask them to enter the things that they would like to have in balance. And, if it is an area the coachee would like to explore, this will make it easier for you to introduce the idea of the 0 point, the fulcrum that is "being" at the centre of mindfulness.

However, more important than questionnaires, wheels of work/life and balances is that the coachee understands the process they are to undertake as the coach's openness about the process brings trust, faith and rapport.

Make an agreement or contract for coaching to begin with confidentiality. This contract needs making with both coachee and client even if it came from the employer of a coachee about a work issue or a life issue.

In my coaching I found that if you are acting to make rapport by using "small talk" then it is false and inhibits depth of openness in responses. It just produces small talk in return, unless the person you are coaching responds only to the use of small talk.

My way to get rapport is to start the session by letting the client freely talk / chat in a non-directive way whilst you unconditionally listen. This builds trust. People value someone who listens to them and this makes them trust the person and have rapport with the person. By not pre-judging coachees you can believe they have huge potential to follow their own map of reality and have good intentions to achieve their objectives perfectly. However, their map of reality is not reality any more than a menu is a meal.

Progressing the coaching process will also increase trust, if you follow an appropriate (to the coachee) amount of relevant structure. And if you judge a coachee then they may deliberately create an opposite of that. Nothing will change. So approach people without judgment, and with empathy. **44)**

Some Skills Used In Creating Rapport

- Be open in how you introduce your coachee to what is coaching
- Ensure that the client knows that they speak with guaranteed confidentiality
- Have a relaxed approach and be approachable
- Show and have respect, trust, integrity
- Be authentic to who you are and what you are doing
- Be sincere and empathic
- Have compassion, open-mindedness and admiration
- Believe in your coachee's potential
- Have clarity of thought, confidence
- Listen effectively

- Be good at establishing your coachee's goal, however, sometimes they just want to talk. So value their just being able to talk about all their options. This is all part of the valuing of the person and building rapport
- Use body language in establishing rapport,such as nodding for listening and mirroring the coachee's sitting position

A Note on Personality Types

A channel of communication with which you can build rapport is language. We can build rapport using a person's language and it also allows us to communicate more effectively with them. People think mainly in pictures, sounds or feelings, and use language which reflects this. **45)** So coaches can use all 3 styles until they understand their coachee and their main mode:

Seeing (visual) e.g. looks like, bright, image, picture.
Hearing (auditory) e.g. hear, sound, wavelength.
Feeling (kinaesthetic) e.g. feel, grasp, sharp, shock.

Further and detailed use of personality profiling tools can further aid this process. E.g. Myers Brigs personality testing. E Extrovert /I Intovert, S Sensing /I Intuition, T Thinking /F Feeling, J Judgment /P Perception. **46)** However, it takes a great deal of skill to use these proficiently. And without this skill the tools will interfere with the coaching process.

5b. Skills - Listening

Listening is a simple skill and yet it is one of the most effective skills for helping focus the coachee on their issues and possibilities. When the coachee is in focus this is a form of mindfulness and the coach's silence, listening and non-judgmentality faciliates the deep opening up of the potential of the coachee's intensive exploration.

So a key skill to help with listening is mindfulness, the focussing of attention in the moment And the use of mindfulness is what keeps the focus and attention on the coachee. It is the way that the coach leads by example as they set their self1 aside and focus completely on the coachee. The coachee can then use this focus if appropriate to their issue. In self 2 the coach removes interference by not trying to get it right, by suspending thoughts, opinions and judgement of the player. **47)**

A person has 1) a teller self and 2) a doer self, this is from the Inner Game, and both coach and client need to be in self 2 where interference doesn't affect performance from potential. **48)** When the coach and the coachee are in an enjoyable awareness there is a "Flow" with clear goal, feedback and concentration. It is "Autotelic" – the activity is its own reward. **49)**

This mindfulness is not no thoughts, it is just noticing what is. We become a still mirror to reflect our client and be a catalyst to the coachee. **50)** Its meditative use depends on what the coachee is comfortable with. And it has an additional use in helping to visualise goals.

Mindfulness helps the coach remain able to give objective help and helps us notice small responses and non-verbal queues, both positive and negative, of coach and coachee that we would miss otherwise. However this mindfulness is not a destination. And in our metaphors the coachee is just allowed to drive where they please, or grow and develop whichever area they think is best.

Although this non-destination relates to Gallwey's self3. Gallwey also describes mindfulness as "mindlessness". Without thinking "the player seems to be immersed in a flow of action…he attempts to exercise control, he loses it." "his mind is so concentrated, so focussed, that it is still. It becomes one…true potential." **51)** But it comes from a state beyond judgment of opposites. Consequently it refers to the ancient Chinese philosophy of the Tao where to be full is to be hollow and vice versa.

Some Skills Used In Having Mindful Listening

- Good use of silence – allowing the coachee to speak
- Listening without judgment - sometimes the coachee just wants to talk. They value just being able to talk about all their options. This is all part of the valuing of the person and rapport building.
- Focussed being in the moment
- Awareness and observation of coachee – and self-awareness
- Detachment from your own responses to the coachee
- Curiosity and patience

A Note on the Use of Meditation

A way to cultivate mindfulness is through meditation - where we can observe our own thoughts, emotions and sensations – just noticing them and not over-thinking. Even noticing that there is part of you that can just notice without being attached to that thought.

A walking meditation is an effective way to experience some of this mindfulness outside of the coaching context. This is where you walk with focus of attention on the walking and not listening to any of the "chattering monkeys" in your mind. Just 10 minutes a few times a week will give you an insight into the process of mindfulness that can help your coaching. You focus on one aspect of your walk, for example; your body, your feet and your toes. Explore how it feels, without letting your attention wander. If a thought intrudes then observe it, do not feel any ownership of the thought, just allow it to happen and then pass. This exercise will help train you in the skill of focussing and will help with focussing on your coachee.

Meditation can help to stimulate better cognitive functioning and increase perceptual accuracy and openness in the coachee. It also breaks down the distinction between self and other. And compassionate meditation can promote more harmonious relationships of all kinds which helps build the coachee's trust so that they open up more. This compassionate approach is more likely to learn and change behaviours and create vision. It is not remedial coaching, focussing on weakness and flaws, but staying with positive stories and showing compassion and not judging the client. **52)**

Liz Hall argues for the use of mindful meditation before a session but I think that not all clients are open to the use of mindfulness meditation. Its use can also lead to a more mindful direction for a client when this isn't necessarily what the client wants. **53)**

I think that mindfulness is inherent within the coaching process and that focus on this is appropriate whereas too much mindfulness becomes meditation, rather than coaching, and can detract from the purpose of the session.

5c. Skills - Feedback

To give more direction to the coaching feedback is required. "Providing feedback is one of the coach's most important skills." **54)**

As the coachee talks it can be useful for the coach to ask pertinent questions. Questions can be used to elicit information. They expand the issue, feeding back to the coachee information below the surface of the volcano. This feedback can be in the form of questions to help explore the coachee's issues. These questions are used to elicit appropriate information and further use Model T to either expand an issue or to focus upon it. By the use of open questions you can help people find their own solutions to complex issues as only they know what those issues are.

Feedback is the coachee's exploration and is augmented with the coach's positive responses, good use of questioning and reflecting back of the coachee's position through summary. By requiring action points (agreed things to be done after the session) the coachee is also given a structured format for development, which can be checked.

Initially I had a very tentative approach in offering feedback to coachees (asking them if this would be acceptable) and I found this to be quite challenging. However, an insight came when I realised that use of summary and repeating back to coachee's was a form of feedback. It was literally feeding back information that they had provided. As such asking questions was also a form of feedback, as it was creating a feedback loop, where the coachee's information created a response by the coach to create further information from the coachee. This helped me approach the philosophical basis of feedback as being less directive (as directive coaching was something I wanted to avoid) and more about facilitating the coachee's journey. And in some ways even silence can also be a form of feedback as it can be used to create additional responses from the coachee when they think that they have said everything they need to on a subject.

Providing clients with feedback is an important coaching technique. It allows the client to discover things about themselves, rather than become fixated on their environment. In its simplest form just repeating, summarising what the person has said can be feedback as it allows coachees to see themselves from another point of view, the interpretative view of the person hearing their feedback.

The 4 tests of whether to offer feedback is; 1. does it raise awareness, 2. does it leave responsibility and choice with the client, 3. does sufficient trust exists between coach and client to make the challenge, 4. is the coach's intent congruent. **55)** I would add a final factor of whether the coachee would like direction or not.

Feedback should come personally from you and be invited by the coachee. You need to agree to discuss the issue and acknowledge sensitivity to the coachee's feelings in this. Then invite the coachee to assess their own performance first. Focus on "skills" and not on the person. Good constructive feedback, that is appropriate and deserved, creates trust and cooperation. It increases skill and improves confidence. Replay to the coachee what they did in a specific situation. Encourage them to highlight the impact of what they did and what they might do even better. Give positive praise for good actions and help them to paint a picture of the desired result. Use specific facts (not generalisations or assumed traits).

However negative feedback – i.e. replaying something that went wrong – is destructive. It creates defensiveness, undermines self-esteem, leaves the person feeling judged. An issue we shall return to later is whether positive feedback also undermines by way of discrepancy based processing. If so then it would imply that feedback (and suggestions) from coach should be neutral, not positive or negative. It is just data. **56)**

A different view to the neutrality of feedback is that feedback should follow PCP, praise-criticism-praise. Be positive, then critical and then finish by being positive again. **57)** As mentioned, being positive gives its own difficulties as we shall see in the Solution Focus section.

Non-the-less the coach should believe in the coachee's potential then they can challenge them to help remove past, limiting beliefs. They should give a suggestion then summarise it amongst all the other options, helping coachees create a picture for future good using mindful visualisation. **58)**

However it is worth noting, in a seeming paradox, that perhaps the most important advice to give to a coach is for them not to give advice.

Mindful Visualisation in Feedback

Mindfulness can be used in Feedback to construct clear images to set the ways forward for a coachee. Use of such visualisation is suggested in many coaching sources e.g. when setting criteria for success imagine seeing, hearing, feeling etc the end point – makes it more vivid and also more precise. **59)**

Visualisation of a goal by a person helps them to achieve it cf Muhammad Ali who would visualise his "Future History". He would picture beating his opponents and even which round he would beat them in. The idea is that if you imagine your future then it strengthens the pathways in your brain which are involved in making an action happen **60)**

Gallwey says that images are better than words for reproducing actions in people. It is a way to show not tell as conscious trying inhibits results. **61)** He continues that the best way for self1 to communicate with self2 is by images and "feelmages." To visualise the result desired and let it happen. He has three kinds of image programming; by results, form and identity. **62)**

Program for Results – have an image of what you want to do, e.g. where you want the ball to go and then allow the body to do what is necessary to do, e.g. hit it there. Trust self2 and let self1 relax. Refrain from giving "how–to-do-it" instructions and a growing confidence will emerge in self2.

Program for Form – give self2 a clear image of the technique you want your body to achieve. Practice in the way you want to performs so your body performs that way. Watch with detachment. Observe and be aware of what is, without judgment, as relaxing is the best precondition for change. Concentration on the object allows the mind to stay in the "now and here" and to let go of self1. For example, the coachee should concentrate on the moving ball, focus on the object. Appreciate the qualities of the object, its shape and texture be fascinated. Listen to the sound, feel the change that they want and feel what it feels like to hit the ball, to hold the racquet, to feel the rhythm. Coachees can also stay concentrated by focussing on breathing (not controlling breathing). **63)**

In this mindset they can "Let it Happen" without conscious control. It is the difference between "making" something happen and "letting" it happen. They don't force it and just observe the results and then re-program where necessary. **64)** If they miss then notice what happened, e.g. where the ball lands. Free of emotional reaction. They don't try, just put faith in their body. Or observe the error in their technique and just notice and feel the changes rather than trying or trying to do it the "right" way. This uses the Groove Theory of Habits. Repeated actions ingrains them as habits. Remove old habits by practicing new ones. **65)**

Program by Identity – this involves role playing in an ideal/professional role. It is imagining and then identifying with that role – this increases the coachee's range of skills.

A similar tool of mindful visualisation is Perceptual Positioning technique which derives from NLP (Neuro Linguistic Programming) and this technique can help in the Programming by Identity. The coachee often has information stored at the unconscious level that can be brought to the surface using the Perceptual Positions. Coachees explore perspectives of their own then step into the shoes of another person in the situation and then into the shoes of a third position of an outside observer (with no emotions involved). **66)**

In exploring the perspective of another person you see yourself as they might see you and this is useful for improving relationships. Then in the third person position further information is uncovered.

The power of perceptual positioning can be enhanced though the use of chairs for seating. The coachee moves from self chair to other chair to the third person chair. Then they stand to comment from the self position but also to show that they have moved on from their original chair. This helps affirm their decision of a way forward.

It is important for your coachee to note that the other person is a phantom construct of their own imagining and requires an appreciation of the limits of your their imagination in trying to understand that other person.

Some Skills Used In Giving Feedback

Being Positive
- Believe in the client's potential
- Be careful of intent when asking questions.
- Be positive and creative
- Have a solution focussed mindset and be detached
- Celebrate success

Challenging
- Challenge and stretch, with honesty and encouragement – raising the bar of possibilities
- Ask powerful questions and allow to answer. Don't use double/multiple questions.
- Ask open questions ("what" and "where" questions that allow developed answers rather than yes and no closed answers)

- If stuck then the coach can say "I don't know the next question, do you?"
- Explore options and look at wider context e.g. ask "what else" and "who else" involved
- Hold the client accountable
- Confront negative behaviours – give feedback
- Influence and help get positive mental attitude
- Review the initial goal so as not to get lost in details
- Encourage the coachee to keep a learning jounal

Respectful of Space
- Repeat and summarise conversations
- Seek permission to offer ideas as suggestions made to coachees tend not to be listened to as they like to make suggestions for themselves.
- Provide appropriate information and feedback
- Delegate tasks and authority depending on what the coachee requires on the Skill/Will Matrix
- Allow small steps to get a way forward
- Don't press for a solution/action, let it evolve and let solutions come between sessions (and/or after sessions) and not require them to come in the session.

Intuitive
- Use intuition and allow for *unexpected factors.*

A Note on Feedback in the Next Session

The process of feedback can carry on in reviewing the current session or at the start of the next session.

You can start your session with an invitation to review e.g. "Show me what you've done..." or "Tell me what you've tried..." "...since the last session." **67)** You should ask the client what is most interesting rather than important or relevant as it creates less interference from value judgments. **68)**

"Of course, the client may not complete the agreed actions exactly as expected. This is simply seen as useful feedback to discover what works. The coach will review the client's actions in subsequent sessions by asking questions such as:

1) What is better?
2) What did you do that made the change happen?
3) What did others do?
4) What have been the effects of the changes?

5) Who else noticed the changes?
6) What do you think will be changing next?" **69)**

However, if your coachee is now comfortable and happy, feels that a real improvement has occurred, has become motivated and / or there has been much dramatic improvement, then they might not yet ready for another session. Instead your coaching session can be more informal. You might spend the session reviewing the actions that they have taken and affirming these actions. Most important is that the focus is on the coachee and not the coach. A whole session spent in review might be needed by a coachee in order to consolidate on learning from the previous session.

Finally, a coach should also seek feedback from the coachee at the end of the session and point out what the coachee has learned from the coaching process to remove any feeling of their dependency.

6. Frameworks For Coaching Sessions

The previous structure for coaching was quite minimal and non-directive, requiring the proficient use of skills by the coach.

To become more ordered and thorough in your coaching it is good to introduce a structure, a framework, however, this isn't to be followed slavishly.

In driving it is like planning a driving routes and what vehicles to use. And in gardening it is like a landscape architect making plans for a gardener's requirements.

Some models are gap analysis where there is a current scenario, preferred scenario and strategies to get there. Some models are quite complex and too detailed and critics would say that the only person who can remember what the acronyms mean is the person who invented the model. However, aspects of complexity can teach about the coaching process but simplicity is best as it allows the coach to be flexible in responding to sessions. **70)**

Sessions can be tightly structured or less structured. The coach needs to be flexible about using structure as a situation demands from the coachee. Coaching is often a non-linear process. A session is uncertain and the coach shouldn't react by clinging to structure. Novices cling to rules, these begin to be seen as loose guidelines and eventually coaches create their own models and move between them, depending on the situation. These bespoke models can become more complex and responsive to complex and novel situations. Eventually the coach is able to understand situations without explicit use of models.

Framework GROW

An effective tool for structuring coaching is the GROW model which was developed by Graham Alexander and several other coaches in the 1980s and was popularised by Sir John Whitmore in "Coaching for Performance" (1992) **71)**

You move through the different stages of the model, however, the model is flexible and you can revisit any of the other stages at any point. This happens in GROW where goals can be redefined and the process end up looking as GRGROGROOGROWOGORW!

Many sources describe the framework. **72) & 73)**

Goal – establish a clear, specific goal, an issue for the session. Agree a topic for discussion and a long term aim if necessary.

Reality – have the coachee describe the current situation without evaluation. Stay detached. Use "Open Questions" to look at Who, What, Where and When, avoiding Why and How. In this stage you should check assumptions and discard irrelevant history.

Options – brainstorm solutions with quantity over quality. Encourage going beyond limits. From these you will be able to choose what to do. And the coach can, carefully, offer suggestions over Options.

Will / What Next? / Way Forward / Wrap up – use questions that support the coachee in considering the options and choosing from them. What are you going to do, when, will this meet your goal, what obstacles might there be, who needs to know, what support do you need, how and when will you get that support. What other considerations do you have. In this stage make steps specific and commit to action with a definite time-frame for objectives, identify possible obstacles and agree support. Ask what degree of certainty the coachee has to carry out the actions. These steps should be SMART (see below).

Many variations of the session structure of the GROW model have emerged e.g. TGROW, I-GROW, SO-I-GROW, CLEAR, OSKAR, ACHIEVE, PRACTICE, OUTCOMES. 74)

The most common of these is TGROW; where Topic was added to the model to establish a general area of discussion. I tend to see the difference between Topic and Goal being a bit like the difference between general strategy and specific tactics. Consequently I prefer not to add the additional T as it can be incorporated into the Goal.

Another variation is RE-GROW, adding that a review of actions from the previous session should be included as part of the structure of coaching sessions to join the sessions up. This means including a short period to Review and Evaluate the learning completed since the last session. However, I think this review and evaluation is a part of the skills of rapport and feedback that are necessary to the general process of coaching and don't necessarily need spelling out in the model.

Extra Framework SMART

SMART is an extra framework that can be added to the "Way Forward" in the general framework of GROW in order to deliver further benefit. SMART is a model used widely in business that can transform a vague goal into something more precise and sharply defined. Below we explain the acronym. **75)**

Specific – Define your goal specifically and narrowly. What do you want? When, where and how?

Measurable – How will you measure success and achievement, i.e. make the goal quantifiable.

Achievable or Agreed – set the goals at the right level, not too easy so that they are a challenge but not too hard to be de-motivating.

Relevant – make sure that the goal is appropriate for the purpose and addresses the problem.

Time bound – decide when the goal will be achieved. If too far off then it isn't motivating, if it is too close then its not worth trying.

In an example of my own SMART small steps concerning a business I was running I considered that in a situation where competitors were targeting my customers that the potential to change myself was greatest but would have the least effect compared with being a change to my competitors having great effect but outside of my capability. I include it here as a chart of change to remind the coach that the coachee's greatest change opportunities lie within themselves.

	Potential to change	*Effect on situation*
Self	*high*	*low*
Customers	*medium*	*medium*
Competitors	*low*	*high*

In our driving metaphor SMART could be seen as knowing the limit of your current driving options for the journeys that you want to make. In gardening it is knowing what is possible to achieve in your garden in the time-frames that you have.

How To Use GROW And SMART

Approach your session using GROW and ask questions such as What is your Goal? What is your Reality? What are your Options? What is your Way Forward?

Use open questions and don't interrupt or talk unnecessarily. Listen well, keep out emotional reactions, keep positive and move from short to long term.

Retain and recap the session.

Remain non-judgmental and do not feel the need to reach a conclusion.

Then add SMART to get the coachee to create specific goals.

Encourage clear direction forward to help guide the coachee and write action points if actions arise.

Solution Focus Principles, Tools & Frameworks; SIMPLE & OSKAR

The difficulty with the GROW and SMART framework is that it is quite unimaginative in operation for the coachee. We have seen how effective imagination can be when powerfully used, in the Inner Game and a framework that has integrated imagination with a positive direction is the Solution Focussed Model. This looks at what's wanted, what's working, progress, strengths, simplicity and actions. This contrasts with Problem Focus which looks at what's wrong, what needs fixing, blame, deficits, weaknesses and complications. **76)**

In driving it is learning how to drive well by not thinking too much about how you drive badly, just practicing driving well. Similarly, in Solution Focus you help your coachee to create an ideal that they aspire towards in small steps, affirming them along the way. In contrast the Inner Game holds the ideal and work towards it with detachment. There is a degree of interference from positive thinking involved in Solution Focus, however, this can be absent in visualised ideals if there is non-attachment to the success or failure of the achievement of that ideal.

In Solution Focus you focus on the positive, however, there are two kinds of positive. The first kind is an ideal that you aim at and the second kind is praise (an affirmation of goodness or worth). There is no interference if the focus is on the ideal and how far a person has achieved that (if this is assessed with balance and non-attachment), however, interference comes if there is blame or praise from self1. And it is self1 that is involved in Solution Focussed coaching.

However, despite reservations, there is a great deal to be gained from the Solution Focussed approach. "Conventionally we assume that learning about the problem will help with working towards a solution. But here, we can see that the problem axis and solution axis are different and independent. Finding out about the problem makes us experts in the problem, which is best overlooked." **77)**

Principles - SIMPLE

The principles of a Solution Focussed approach can be spelled out in the acronym SIMPLE. **78)**

Solutions Not Problems - Focus on solutions avoids wasting time on problem talk.

In-between – solutions often rest between people and their interactions. So we should look at peoples actions in context to promote helpful interactions. Although don't look for deeper hidden issues that are not there.

Make Use Of What's There – look for the seeds of the solution in what has happened before or is developing already. Find positive counters and don't look for deficits.

Possibilities – use stories from the past, explanation of the present or vision of the future. Avoid accusations and use resourceful words. Generate positive expectations.

Language – use simple $5 words and not over complex $5,000 words. Also make sure that you both understand what is meant by a term. Be specific with descriptions and quantifications in language.

Every Case is Different – Solution Focus is an approach and not a fixed method. You construct bespoke solutions to fit each unique situation. Let the solution come and not be forced. Have a "beginner's mind" that is open to new possibilities. Don't seek big solutions as small actions can make a quick difference and show the way of what works.

At this point it is worth restating that the Inner Game philosophy is potentially against SIMPLE because the former views positive thinking as potentially hindering progress as much as negative thinking. Positive thinking sets up a standard and an expectation that keeps the person from correct functioning, e.g. ladies hitting balls into the net were more successful when there wasn't any praise as self1 sees a compliment as a potential future criticism if a standard is not achieved. "compliments are criticism in disguise! Both are used to manipulate behaviour, and compliments are just more socially acceptable!" 79) This links back to the problems of discrepancy based processing where there is a tendency to get depressed if too high a goal is set. 80)

Although the difference may be semantic there are two aspects to Solution Focus. As I don't think these are spelled out in the literature I will try and separate out their functions. One is the focus on what works, which can be a purely practical matter and not produce interference. The other is an emotive evaluation, e.g. "that's great!" or "well done, that's really good" which can produce distracting pressure. As such any praise or criticism offered has to be objective as possible so that the coachee sees it as a practical evaluation rather than emotive.

The positive affirmation should be about doing the ideal way of doing actions (like Program for Results) and not self1 evaluative judgments of good and bad of the person and their abilities. This is a focus on the ideal without being attached to progress towards it or regression from it. It affirms the ideal and describes the ideal and merely states any progression or regression made. Affirming the progress made or the person can give interference and can be distracting from the task or create confusion.

Affirmation seems to fit more with motivation theory, and affirmation is at the top of the employee's ranking for aspects of work that they want (with good wages being the top aspect that employers mistakenly think that employees want). **81)** This affirmation leads to the employee being happier in the job and more motivated to act – however, it is part of discrepancy based processing and is not necessarily the result of a coaching process. None-the-less it can be useful for pinnacle coaching.

In addition, the Solution Focus also has a number of imaginative and positive "tools" that are quite specific and make the Solution Focussed process very structured. And they can also be adapted and used in different frameworks once their functions are understood. **82)**

Tools

The Platform – this is a solid place, a foundation, from where the coachee starts and "departs" from a problem. This can be derived from the problem but it is important not to get stuck in problem talk. Make sure that the problem is solvable and that the coachee is a customer for change. This foundation does not need visualising, rather it is a term to denote your coachee's solid starting point.

Future Perfect – here we use visualisation to make an imaginary leap to the situation without the problem as if the problem went away overnight, e.g. imagine a miracle has happened and what small signs can the coachee see? Have the coachee describe the scene.

Counters – things that count in getting the coachee to the solution – resources, skills, know-how and expertise. Aspects of the Future Perfect already happening or that have happened before times that the problem wasn't there, resources and skills they already have or have used all of these helpers can be imagined as "counters" with a points value that will help the coachee to reach their solution.

Scaling – a form of scaling can be imagined (taking the coachee from their worst case scenario to their ideal scenario) and the counters can be placed along that scale to help show where the coachee is. This is typically the 1to10 pinnacle scaling.

Affirming – this is being positive in recognising and valuing what is already contributing towards the coachee's solution. Compliment the coachee and draw their attention to what is working already. This affirmation can also be used at many points in the process of coaching.

Small Actions – small, well chosen actions can make a big difference. Note the positive difference that they make and then take further actions from this new point.

Framework - OSKAR

Once the principles and tools of Solutions Focussed coaching are understood then the most effective use of the OSKAR framework can be made. OSKAR is a framework that helps the coaches ask general questions (like GROW) but also uses specific techniques at each stage. OSKAR is useful as it is a kind of story and helps the coachee create a narrative of their life, however, other stories could be constructed.

Outcome – here the "Platform" is established. What are the coachee's objectives and what do they want to achieve today and in the long-term. How do these tie in with what a client (e.g. manager or coachee themselves) might want. Then the "Future Perfect" (the Dream/Vision beyond the normal) is imagined.

Scaling – the coachee is asked where on a scale of "1to10", they are today? Affirm the coachee in having reached the point that they have reached as this means that they are already part of the way to their goal. "Great! What can get you further up the scale?"

"Whatever the client offers, the coach will affirm them for having achieved that much. Even a 1 is on the scale, so the coach may ask, "Great! What are you doing that means you get to be on the scale?" Anything higher than 1 obviously provides more opportunity for affirming the client in what they are already doing, to have been as successful as they are in getting that high." **84)**

At this point the coach can explore how did they get there? How would they know that they had got an extra point up the scale?

It is important to note that the traditional scaling of OSKAR is 1-10, reflecting a directive, goal, achievement, Doing orientation and not a consideration of the -5to+5 scale of Being.

Although **83)** says that it doesn't matter if the scale starts at 0 or at 1. In order to have a relationship to balance scaling it should start at 0, c.f. The Sturges Triangle.

Know How and Resources – from this point the coach attempts to progress the solution by asking what "counters" helps the coachee perform at the number they are at the scale rather than at number 0/1? They also ask what being further up the scale would look like and if / when does the outcome happen already and how did they do / achieve that?

Affirm and Action – next they ask what's already going well and "affirm" the coachee in their success? Then they discover the small actions, the next small steps that it would take to get the coachee an extra point up the scale? At any point they "affirm" the coachee to motivate them. However, as mentioned, there is a danger that this "Affirming" is positive thinking, which distorts the mind from seeing things as they are as much as negative thinking. **85)** It produces a directive, goal orientated mindset, which is fine if that is the kind of coaching required.

Any small actions set should be SMART **86)** and the benefit of OSKAR is that it makes them more personal to the performer (through use of imagery) than the more abstract SMART used in GROW alone.

Review – here you look at what has changed for the coachee. What's better? What did they do to make the change happen? What effects have the changes had? What will they change next? The purpose is to seek progress. Ask how has it been achieved and in what direction does it point. Also ask how it can be maintained or improved.

A number of my coachees preferred GROW to OSKAR as they like to work with generality and OSKAR created a long list of actions – that was too specific and too many. The model also uses a good deal of visualisation and care needs taking to include auditory and kinaesthetic descriptions in these.

The model, nonetheless, provides a good way to create ways forward that can be visualised. However, there are limits to what can be imagined constructively as possibilities. Living in fairyland castles or exploring planets in spaceships would be unrealistic visualisations. However, the non-judgmental coach should allow their coachees to have these visions, without constraining them, as out of them might come some practical options that could be fulfilled e.g. renovating a house or learning to be a pilot.

In Driving – this might be seen as the small steps that the coachee takes as they descends from the coach to their destination. The coach picks the traveller up from their current location then, with the aid of a map or ideal blue-print, carries the traveller into the mountains, forests, lakes and rivers and from there they must make the rest of their journey on foot. Or in the case of the original term of "coach" the Oxford student arrives in London where they descent to go on their career journey into "city life" after university.

In gardening this is working out how you want your garden to look but only expecting a small amount of growth at each stage.

The idea of only taking small steps led to me thinking of the clichéd proverb that a journey of a thousand miles begins with a single step. However, in mindfulness it continues with a single step, and is only ever a single step at a time. However, the directive, pinnacle goal based nature of OSKAR and SMART and the other frameworks can restrict the non-directive, balancing mindful essence of the coaching process. They can set goals too far and too high. I intuitively felt that another model was required to reflect non-directive mindfulness, and for this reason I developed the GROWFLOW model which we shall look at in the next chapter.

7. The GROWFLOW Frameworks for Coaching

In the course of coaching I noticed a number of similarities in the diverse models used. I've tried to incorporate a number of these into the GROWFLOW model including; GROW, OSKAR, Will/Skill and Change-House. The model also makes use of SIMPLE, SMART, Inner Game Programming and a mindfulness technique named FEEL.

The first thing to note is that GROW is concerned with pinnacle goals, FLOW is concerned with balance and GROWFLOW is a combination of the two. However, before we look at FLOW we will look at how GROW maps directly onto the Change House and Will / Skill Matrix.

Earlier in the book we mapped how the Change House fit onto the Will / Skill Matrix. So we have also mapped GROW onto both the Will / Skill Matrix and the Change House. The movement around the model is anti-clockwise.

Contentment Guide hw/hs Goal	Renewal Delegate lw/hs Way
Denial Direct hw/ls Reality	Confusion |Excite lw/ls Options

Goal / Contentment – the coachee is content in having reached their goal and has high will and skill. Goal is the point where the coachee has high achievement and motivation but moves to recognising new skills and the need for guidance, education and learning.

Reality / Denial – the coachee doesn't want to accept that their contentment is now problematic, they still have high will but now have a skill deficit. Reality is the situation of the coachee's lack of skills to address a new (or current) problem are shown to the coachee and the direction they will need to take over how to train in a new areas, however, this may result in demotivation.

Options / Confusion – with so many options there is confusion and de-motivation. Options are the overwhelming possibilities are gradually given shape and the coachee becomes proficient in them. The coachee needs exciting over which options are best to choose.

Way / Renewal – the way forward brings a renewal and a new direction. This creates optimism and enthusiasm for the new development of skills. Way is the choices that can be made by the coachee who has now become motivated to act as they become more in control of the situation. They can then be delegated more duties.

However the mapping needs adapting to fit the progression through the changes. So we split the stages of the Matrix into the Will / Skill state of the person and the Will / Skill method used to progress them to the next stage. We map the Will / Skill stage onto GROW and rotate that 90 degrees clockwise, putting the goal as the pinnacle.

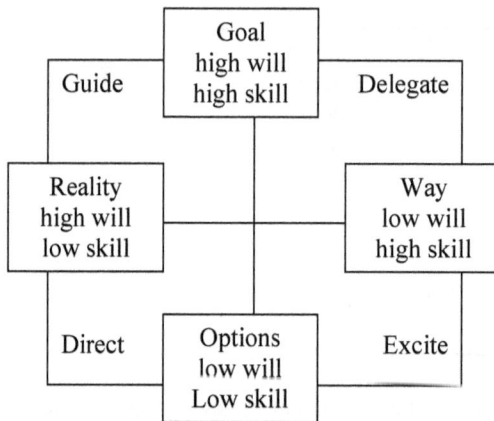

	Goal high will high skill	
Guide		Delegate
Reality high will low skill		Way low will high skill
Direct	Options low will Low skill	Excite

From here we begin to see the emergence of FLOW as the way to move between the stages of GROW. GROWFLOW coaching recognises that the activity of coaching is naturally mindful in its own right, if done properly and is a meditiative state. **87)** As such it moves away from directive structures and is even more mindful if based in FLOW.

However, the way that we define FLOW is in relationship to GROW. And you should start your coaching with GROW and then add FLOW as you get more experienced. FLOW is more intangible than GROW as it is the processes of moving between the stages of GROW that get neglected.

It is coaching between the gaps. FLOW is the road (or river) between the destinations. It is the journey itself, rather than the destinations, the towns or road-marks of GROW.

The important difference between GROW and FLOW is between Doing and Being (or rather allowing yourself to be in a state of "becoming"). GROW looks at the Product, the quantitative stages, and is directive towards an object. In contrast FLOW looks at the Process, the qualitative movement between stages and is non-directive through that process. In GROWFLOW you choose which of the 2 approaches to focus upon GROW or FLOW or to have a combination of the 2 in GROWFLOW. Whether you focus on achieving outcomes / doing outcomes or on being / becoming will determine the approach that you take.

Another way to look at it is that GROW is finding and fulfilling the needs of self1 whereas FLOW is finding and fulfilling the needs of self2. It is pinnacle Doing in contrast to balanced Being.

On its own FLOW coaching is focussed on how the coachee wants to Be and not on what they want to Do. This is less about specific goals and more based in being and allowing issues to arise, expand and then organise themselves into ways of being. The perfection of FLOW is in self3, in high skill with no will. The coachee can abandon will here and "go with the flow" (although this is not a goal as such, it is more the removal of a need to have a goal).

The acronym FLOW stands for Find, Learn, Organise and Work.

Find how or who you want to Be.

Learn what you need to Be that person.

Organise ideas of that person into your identity, your Being.

Work as that person, that Being.

An example of just FLOW is as follows:

Find – " I want to be happy and have meaning."
Learn – "I have happiness in work and my personal life and also problems that come from other people and also my own reactions to those other people."

Organise – "I will put working on my own reactions first as I can control these and take responsibility for them."
Work – "I am happier now that I realise that perceived problems are actually from my own reactions."

Find (a new way to be or destination) – here we use the skills of hypothesising, to guide our coachee to teach and present to themselves evidence of new realities about how they may need to change their outlooks, directions or skills. Our coachee explores how they want to be and the discrepancy between that and who they are, e.g. "I want to find meaning in my life" implying the discovery of a lack of meaning.

Learn (about obstacles on the way) – here we look at the evidence and reality in more detail, our coachee's responses to it and options around it. We "direct" our coachee through their doubts and overwhelming possibilities. This is directive but not towards a fixed end goal. It is "direction" in a way committed to the learning process of authentic discovery, not hiding behind illusions of selves. Our coachee sees who they are, in more detail, e.g. "I like working, walking and helping people."

Organise (the ideal self or route to that self) – here we look at the results of the coachee's searching journey and help excite them to organise their options into a persuasive perspective that they will feel ownership of. One that will empower them with a sense of readiness to engage with the outside world. Make this their way forward. It is a way for the coachee to sift through their possible selves to find the one that they wish to become and the one that will work for them, e.g. "I want to spend more time feeling that I'm helping people with less time feeling stressed."

Work (become and be the destination) – here our coachee takes an overview of their new perspective and begins to perform with it as a basis for underpinning who they are. Then they can delegate their tasks to this new self. Our coachee becomes their possible self, e.g. "I am focussing on the parts of my life where I get value and meaning from helping people."

It is in this section that we can use the most important addition to the model. This is the framework FEEL which is a way to visualise the specific, small steps of SMART. FEEL, formed by Liz Hall 88), stands for Focus, Explore, Embrace, Let Go. And onto this I map the Program of Results, Form and Identity of Gallwey's Inner Game.

Focus (visualise your small steps) - Program by Results (what to do),

Explore (make the image clearer) - Program by Form (technique to use),

Embrace (identify with this image of your future self) - Program by Identity (person to be),

Let Go (do not be attached to the image). Coachees can become quite attached to their ideal visions of small steps so the Letting Go is softened so that coaches can release their vision, leave it and return to who and where they are at the present moment. Returning with detached compassion towards their possible future self. **"Let it happen", "Let it be"** – are other ways to term this acting without conscious control, without forcing it.

However, if the coachee is using GROWFLOW and has chosen to have a more directive and goal focussed coaching then instead of Letting Go the person can be more active in the process and Take from that visualisation a more conscious control of the small steps forward. This becomes **FEET** which is more directive as it is linked to the small steps.

It is interesting to note that as well as being part of "Work" FEEL also corresponds with FLOW only it is more detailed and specific and uses more visualisation whereas FLOW establishes generalities;

Find – Focus
Learn – Explore
Organise (Own) – Embrace
Work (Allow to work) – Let Go

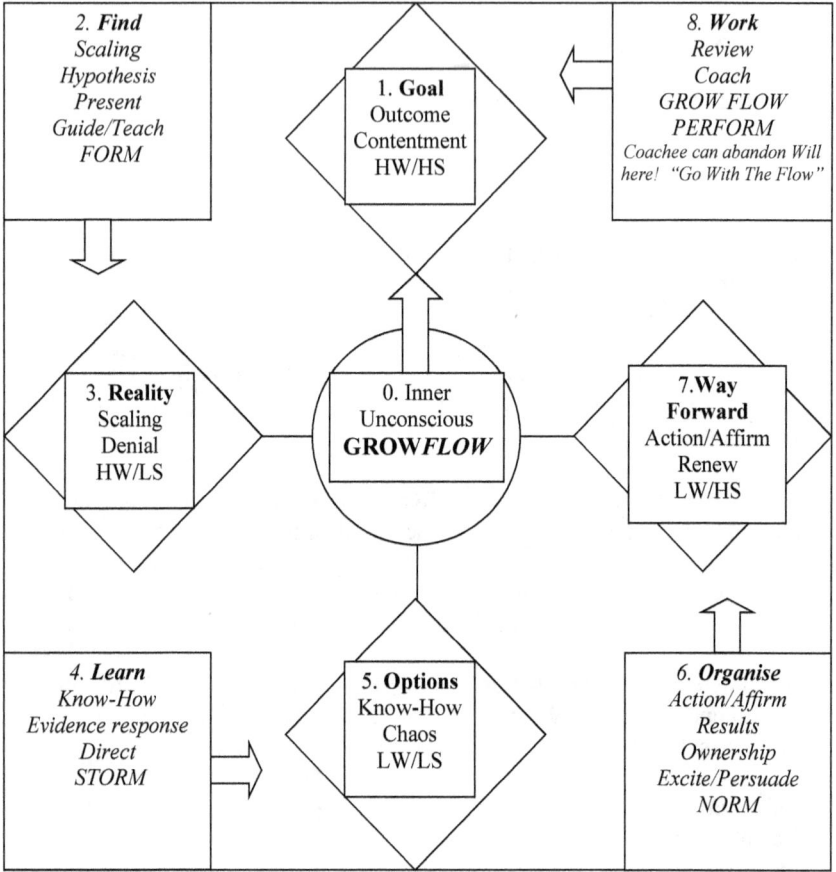

2. Find
Scaling
Hypothesis
Present
Guide/Teach
FORM

1. Goal
Outcome
Contentment
HW/HS

8. Work
Review
Coach
GROW FLOW
PERFORM
Coachee can abandon Will
here! "Go With The Flow"

3. Reality
Scaling
Denial
HW/LS

0. Inner
Unconscious
GROW*FLOW*

7.Way
Forward
Action/Affirm
Renew
LW/HS

4. Learn
Know-How
Evidence response
Direct
STORM

5. Options
Know-How
Chaos
LW/LS

6. Organise
Action/Affirm
Results
Ownership
Excite/Persuade
NORM

GROWFLOW Mapped Onto OSKAR

Next GROW and GLOW can be put together into GROWFLOW can also be mapped onto the OSKAR model;

G	F	R	L	O	O	W	"W"
O	S	S	K	K	A	A	"O"

1 - Goal Outcome (GO) – Affirm the coachee in who and where they are. Asses their goal and establish that GROWFLOW coaching is to be about a Mindful approach or a Directive approach. In Mindfulness the Goal is just to be, in a Flow State. In a directive approach the goal is to achieve an action. In a repeat session reassess and review the goal and determine if it is achieved or needs work and is the topic for the current session.

2 - Find Scaling (FS) – scaling – look for your coachee's new ideal goal, situation or way of being to see what needs doing to reach it.

3 - Reality Scaling (RS) – use scaling (pinnacle or balance) to show the current reality versus the ideal situation, to give evidence of a shortfall in reaching the ideal but not options. The coachee needs affirmation as they may enter a state of discomfort, uncertainty and denial if support isn't offered.

4 - Learn Know How (LK) – look at what is currently working

5 - Options Know How (OK) – expand the options and look at other things working for other people, times, places etc. when has it worked better, what are the other possibilities.

6 - Organise Action Affirm (OA) – affirm and summarise the options to give ownership to the coachee so that they can organise their thoughts and options.

7 - Way Forward Action Affirm (WA) – let the coachee come up with an action – the way forwards – the small steps

8 - Work Outcome (WO) – the coachee now visualises the small steps and uses FEEL.

We have put the acronyms into a story to make it more memorable.

1 - Goal Outcome	GO
2 - Find Scaling	FiSh
3 - Reality Scaling	ReSt
4 - Learn Know How	LooK
5 - Options Know How	OKay
6 - Organise Action Affirm	OArs
7 - Way Forward Action Affirm	WAy
8 - Work Outcome	WOrk

Crusoe GOes FiShing!
Robinson Crusoe, stuck on a desert island was quite happy. When Man Friday arrived he realised that they needed bigger fish to survive.
Man Friday told him to "**GO, FiSh**."
Crusoe had a **ReSt** to evaluate his situation.
He had a **LooK** around to see what he had used to catch food before.
He considered his options and began to realise that he would be **OKay**.
He would make a small coracle and organise his fishing trip by rowing with **OArs**.
This was the **WAy** forward.
This would **WOrk** to help Crusoe reach his Goal.
A nutritious meal!

Your General Approach In Coaching With GROWFLOW.

First focus on the coachee and make the process all about them. Establish rapport through conversation and through focus on the coaching process by letting the coachee know that your focus is completely on them. Next give the coachee a choice about the directive or non-directive coaching that they wish to use and a choice about their scaling to that purpose.

Gain proficiency in the GROWFLOW model so that you can use it in a freer way, for a seamless use of coaching skills and styles. Aim to listen to the coachee and let them progress in their own time. 30 minutes to 1 hour is a good length of time for a session.

At each stage the coachee may prefer to use GROW or FLOW dynamics or both. GROWFLOW gives you the flexibility to adapt to the coachee's needs.

Listen attentively and hold a space, allowing the coachee to describe the current situation and to follow through trains of thought before adding any elements through open questions. Compare this to a situation or way of being that had worked previously or if past situations aren't strictly comparable then examine possible combinations of scaling and balances then look at a small step to ensure balance.

Encourage the coachee to take a SMART small step forward. Then have the coachee visualise a Goal with FEEL connecting to that Goal or Being or to evolve to a small step after the session.

GROWFLOW In Problem And Solution Focussed Dialogue

As you progress in using GROWFLOW you may find times when you are in Problem or in Solution focussed dialogues. The aim is to transform the conversation between the coach and the coachee from a problem focussed dialogue for the coachee to a co-operative solution focussed dialogue for both the coach and the coachee. This will involve both in a co-operative dialogue at each stage of the process, rather than oppositional and alternating between stages.

In Problem Focussed Dialogue

In a Problem Focus the GROWFLOW model is like a dialogue between the coachee who represents a resistant normal self1 (1,3,5,7) and the coach who represents a persistent higher self2 (2,4,6,8), moving the coachee from stage to stage. The Inner Unconscious (0, centre of diagram) produces an expressive dynamic into (1) (like the core of the earth producing a volcano out of the earth's crust). The coach / self2 presents this as a Finding/Hypothesis (2) that moves (if not blocked by the coachee / self1) through the stages 1-8 until reaching the Goal again (like the lava and the surface of the volcano cooling). The overall Goal is a process of effective growing and flowing in harmony without blockages (although new issues can arise often creating their own volcanoes).

Coachee - **1. Goal/Contentment – "I reached the Goal! I'm the best."**

Coach - 2. Finding/Hypothesis – "There's something you can develop. How can you get your solution even better to reach your ideal?"

Coachee - **3. Reality/Denial – "There's no problem."**

Coach - 4. Learn/Evidence – "Here's proof you still need to develop."

Coachee - **5. Options/Chaos – "I accept there's things I need to do, but there are many possibilities that I don't know what to do."**

Coach - 6. Organise/Persuade – "Okay, what are your best (SMART) options to take you to your ideal?"

Coachee - **7. Way Forward/Renew – "I choose to do this action. And whilst you have helped me I have come up with the solution."**

Coach - 8. Work/Coach – "How will you do that action or Be that person best? FEEL the result. And what other issues arise from this?"

In Solution Focussed Dialogue

A Solution Focussed, collaborative dialogue occurs between the coach and coachee at each of the stages of GROWFLOW from 1-8 (rather than an alternating at each stage). At each stage self1 and self2 co-operate. At any part the coach can recognise if the coachee needs to use GROW or FLOW or to continue in GROWFLOW.

Coach – 1. You are great in where you are (even if they haven't achieved their previous goals). Take time to affirm yourself and to appreciate who you are. You are completely fine and good in your goals.
Coachee – **1. 'I have reached the Goal.'**

Coach – 2. 'That's working. What is your next ideal or Goal? How else do you want to Be? Please describe it.' Determine if the coachee wants to progress up a scale or to reach a balance in a scale.
Coachee – **2. Describes their next Goals / ways of Being.**

Coach – 3. 'Where on a scale (of 0to10 or -5to+5) are you in relation to it?'
Coachee – **3. – 'I am here.' Describes scale and the reality.**

Coach – 4. 'It's great you are so far up the scale or you are working effectively to get near to a balance. What practice or ways of being are currently working for you?'
Coachee – **4. - Describes their good or effective practice or Being.**

Coach – 5. 'These practices provide some good options. Lets expand them and look at what has worked for people (self and others), times (past and present) and places (here and elsewhere).'
Coachee – **5. - Describes other good or effective practice or Being.**

Coach – 6. 'That's a good or effective set of options? Which would you like to take?'
Coachee – **6. – 'I wish to take this option.'**

Coach – 7. 'From these options which SMART small steps would you like to use to take this forward, to move you just 1 up the scale?'
Coachee – **7. – 'I wish to do or Become this.'**

Coach – 8. 'How do we implement this? Visualise this and use the FEEL model (Focus, Explore, Embrace and Let Go). Let's Review. How can you get your solution even better? Are there any new issues arising from this.'

Coachee – 8. – **Coachee reviews, then, using GROWFLOW again, they may go into the "Fractal Flow" with new issues arising from 0. Alternatively the session may end naturally. 8 can also be used to take the process back to 1 where the coachee then takes time to reaffirm themselves before exploring the next issue.**

The fractal FLOW is the review at the end of coaching GROWFLOW, to see if the issue requires deeper coaching. This can take you deeper and deeper into an issue, staying in mindful attention and focus. The term "Fractal" comes from organic, mathematical model zooming into the smaller branches and sub-branches or a form / structure. The branches of the smaller structure reflecting the larger structure and so on in an infinite progression / replication whether you zoom smaller or larger.

8. A Definition of Coaching Culture

The relationship between coaching and business often determines its value, it is, however, of value as an activity in itself and in this final section I would like to suggest why this needs appreciating if there is to be a meaning and a place for the term "coaching culture".

How cultural you see coaching as will depend on whether you focus on it as developing a person towards directive peak goals or in a life-balancing. If coaching is pinnacle goal orientated then coaching is less a culture in itself, and more like a tool, like a phone or a typewriter, only a management tool. Any culture can use this tool, whether Amazonian Indians, Chinese businesspeople or American sportspeople.

However, coaching can also form a more substantial part of a culture if it is given greater importance than being a mere tool. The main manifestation of coaching as a culture comes out of mindfulness where the coaching is used for self actualisation and personal, spiritual, development.

Some would argue that there are a number of assumptions implicit in coaching that link it to such a spiritual cultural perspective, as we have seen Zen Buddhism or Taoism. However, some of the core skills and tools in coaching are significantly shared between cultures to constitute the description of being trans-cultural. As such they might mistakenly remain viewed as being tools even when used more extensively than originally designed to be used in an indigenous culture.

I'd like to suggest that people confuse the different modes of coaching, mixing up "being" with "doing". I believe that to seek a pinnacle goal-orientated benefit for non-dual, non-directive coaching undermines it. It is a way of Being and benefits come as a by-product of it. To seek benefits from it makes it inauthentic as a culture.

So, the use of coaching in a business culture can either be as a tool or as a lifestyle approach or both. And the degree to which you use the coaching determines its effect.

Culture and business are structured activities that are directive and this fits with directive coaching. Whereas non-directive coaching, without structure, contrasts with this and you cannot easily change people from a business, instrumental coaching mindset to a focus on non-directive being.

A Coaching Culture might have more direct usefulness than other cultural forms that you might have in the offices of your business, e.g. the arts of painting, sculpture and music. Coaching can be used to help solve problems directly affecting a business, however, coaching also has some of the same benefits as art in the offices. The arts can have benefits of greater feelings of wellbeing and creativity that are indirectly useful. And there are many similarities in the way that those benefits are produced. There is good art and bad art. And the effect that the art has can depend on where you hang it.

Similarly, there is good coaching and bad coaching and its effect can depend on where you use it in the organisation. Whether those using it are receptive to it or not. And the more superficial its use then the more easily accepted it is but the less effect it has.

If coaching is cultural then it is a cultural activity rather than the content of a culture and as such shouldn't need to replace the whole culture. Trying to "create a coaching culture" is perhaps the wrong approach, whereas "including coaching within the current culture" might better describe the situation. If a coaching culture is pitted against a business culture then I believe that it will, at best, be assimilated without any radical change.

It is this tension between the tool (doing) and the culture (being) of coaching and the results that it gets for businesses which helps create extra problems in defining its proper use in business. It is a tension between business leaders who want coaching to be a tool in their standard business use and those that want it to transform business culture.

The individual resistance to coaching discussed in the earlier chapters, on the basis of it being all based on will, also apply in business. If a case for its use as a skill or tool can be made then it might be accepted. However, debate between the competing viewpoints is often without connection as both start from different assumptions and premises.

So there is a human element involved that is not strictly rational. In effect what is required is a tipping point. And if this doesn't come from overwhelming proof of a case for coaching then change might only occur through members of the dominant corporate culture leaving or being replaced.

4 key differences between coaching and business cultures are over;

Directness - to the point vs implying a message

Hierarchy – following orders vs debate and relationships

Consensus – dissent accepted vs unanimity needed

Individualism – individual winners vs teamwork **99)**

The problem is that when coaching derives its value from Return on Investment ROI and is justified in terms of exterior values instead of having clearly demonstrable value in itself then the coaching has less inherent value. However, if the coach doesn't make ROI the main consideration then they might miss the point for that company. In effect they are speaking a different language and the coach is not contracting goals effectively for the client.

A Directive Coaching Culture

An example of coaching as a business tool is Command Control Coaching (CCC), a fictional model of an inauthentic culture where coaching is manipulatively used for business ends. It is not a genuine model to be used.

It has 3 levels, the "Boss", the Managers and the Workers. The "Boss" is sold the value of coaching for its "return on investment" (ROI) with the person orientated returns of coaching being reduced to being financially orientated. Standard benefits of coaching get transformed where;

More staff job satisfaction for coached staff becomes Less need for pay rises and more loyalty.

Greater Efficiency of staff becomes Improved costs.

More openness about problems and solutions becomes Gaining insider information.

And the Good Public Relations that using coaching might have becomes about Better Sales

Built into the CCC model is that managers are responsible for coaching only the workers in their own divisions and this keeps the various groups of workers and managers separate. However the workers have a coach amongst them who will report back to a manager and to the "Boss" via the "Snitch Line". The managers also coach each other and just one of these managers (will also report back about the other to the "Boss" via the "Snitch Line"). The "snitch" worker and manager are also expected to coach and "snitch" on each other.

It's difficult to align an organisation's inner value with individual workers' and bosses' values. Our values have no substance or logic if not from inner systems. So, ultimately, for a coach, the change is a gradual process of developing and testing hypothesis – about a person or organisation. And the coach needs to notice, formulate and test if the hypothesis is correct. As the coaching occurs in an organisational context the coach may need to report to that organisation/client to meet its needs. **100)** So whilst our example of a "Snitch Line" takes reporting to an unreasonable level the correct level for this reporting needs addressing in the contracting stage of coaching.

In general, this top-down leadership focuses on technical problem solving imposed from top down and only works in a non-competitive environment. In competitive environments adaptive change is required. Staff need to be able to revise beliefs, actions and values and then respond to the external environment experimentally with a plan of action. They need to move from the passive "You want me to do it" to the active "I want to do it."

It is natural to want to be technical or evasive in solutions but we need to be adaptive and creative. The group also needs to want to have this change in approach and coaching helps people with this adaptive approach. **101)**

The basic argument remains, that in order to survive in a competitive environment then both businesses and individuals would do well to embrace coaching.

Figure 8a. A Directive Coaching Culture

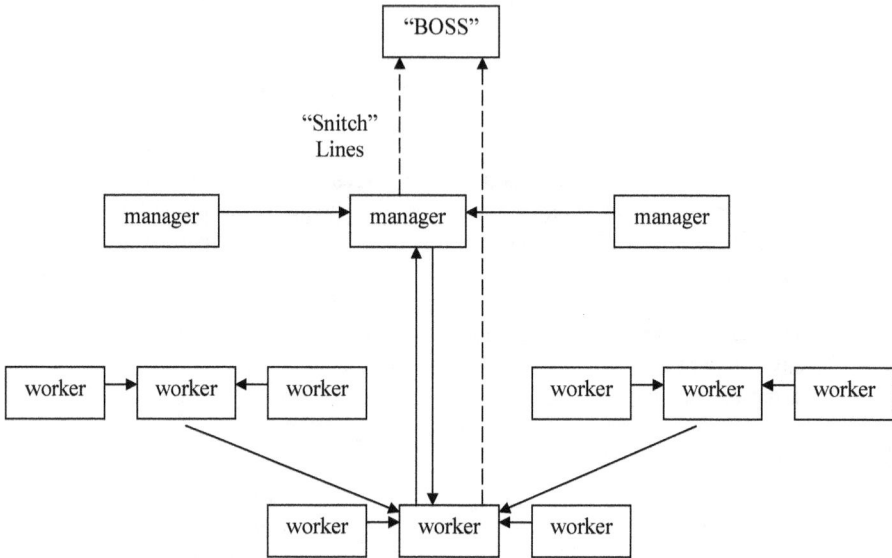

Figure 8b. Authentic Coaching Culture

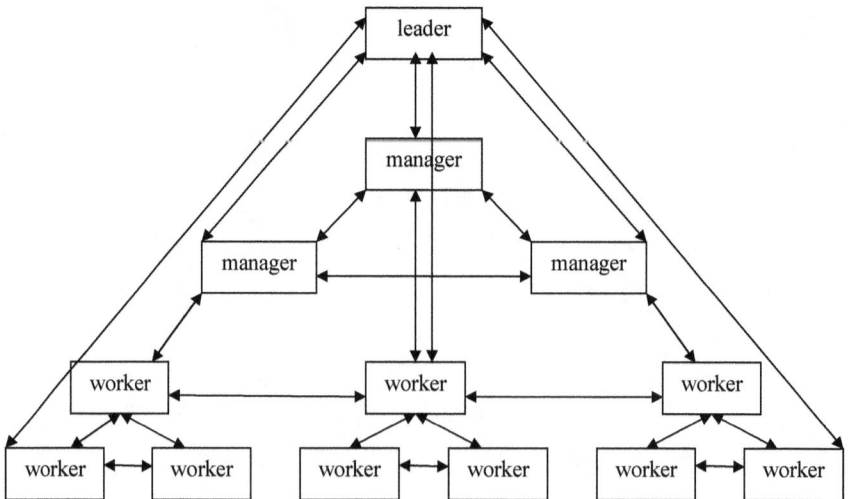

Authentic Coaching Culture

Just like with individual clients coaching for business is a balance between directive, pinnacle goals and non-directive balance, depending on the circumstance.

In contrast to the CCC coaching for control is coaching for developing skills and attitude. It is not about blame instead it concerns creating collective goals and involves everyone equally (not authority, power or control). it is about being an entrepreneur and not a "Boss". **102)**

However, it is problematic whether/or how far coaching can be imposed top down or needs to form from the bottom up. If from the bottom up it is authentic, but if from the top down it is directive.

In order to create a coaching culture Megginson and Clutterbuck have described Four stages towards creating a coaching culture, Nascent, Tactical, Strategic and Embedded **103)**

Nascent – Where there is little or no commitment to creating a coaching culture. Where coaching is used (if at all) for status by executives and not for addressing deep issues. Here there is no strategy for its use and the coaches used might be poor in their skills.

Tactical – Where leaders see value in a coaching culture but don't understand what it means or what will be involved.

Strategic – Where managers and employees are educated about the value of coaching.

Embedded – Where people at all levels are engaged both formally and informally in coaching between functions and levels. Includes 360 degree feedback.

If we imagine an organisation to be like a person then I think that this is like GROW, only arranged in a different order, as ROWG;

Nascent is the Reality from which the organisation wants to move.

Tactical is the Options that are being spelled out concerning the use of coaching in organisations.

Strategic is the Way Forward and the steps by which the whole organisation can adopt a coaching culture.

Embedded is the Goal fulfilled where the coaching is now used throughout the organisation.

However, whilst you can coach an individual the coaching of a whole organisation is a more complex endeavour. A standard model for change that could be employed to aid with a paradigm shift is that of Tuckman's Model of Team Dynamics. This is the Forming, Storming, Norming and Performing. 104)

This basically argues that a team Forms, its competing members Storm, then a consensus is achieved which becomes the team's Norm and from this point they can Perform as a team, until the next round of Forming begins.

1. Forming	4. Performing
2. Storming	3. Norming

This fits how a company would become a coaching organisation as it also fits with a GROW model, being the FLOW between each stage of GROW. It looks at how the organisation wants to "Be".

1. Goal
2. Forming (Find)
3. Reality
4. Storming (Learn)
5. Options
6. Norming (Organise)
7. Way
8. Performing (Work)

The whole organisation needs involving in this FLOW coaching process. And it is less concerned with goals and more focussed on processes. Less on what people in the organisation would like to "do" and more about how they would like to "be", on how the organisation would like to "be".

The aim would be to create something more akin to a more collaborative model of a coaching culture. This would have 2 way directional arrows between all levels of the organisation. It would have the facility for workers to report directly to the CEO / leader.

Cultural Diversity

At this point it is important to note that coaching as a culture isn't strictly neutral. Coaching, particularly with mindfulness, has a distinct mystical component that can be at odds with the values of more moralistic, dualistic, monotheistic faiths – where good and evil are in a fundamental conflict. Eastern religions are viewed as idolatrous and underpinned by heretical, pantheistic and / or mystical philosophies. N.B. not-with-standing the influence of the current non-dualistic mystical revivals in these traditions, e.g. Christian Mysticism or Islamic Sufism. Also not-with-standing that many mystical faiths operate in a hierarchical, directive manner.

We spoke of the martial artist swordsperson who becomes one with their weapon. And of the Zen archer who practices without attachment to the results. These traditions link to Zen Buddhism and mindfulness as individual, non-directive practices. And just as a person can function in tune with their weapon so also they can function in tune with their social role.

In the Hindu Bhagavad Gita, Arjuna (an incarnation of the God Krishna) stands in his chariot with his bow and arrow. He discusses his role as a warrior and the fulfilment of his destiny, Karma, through a mindful focus on his task. He argues that the different social castes function effectively at the levels they are created for. This hierarchy can be quite inflexible. And coaching in Business organisations / Society is more Hindu than Buddhist, where workers and managers are in their set roles. Only the Leader, the Brahmin / Priest in Hinduism can seek full Buddhist style enlightenment. Similarly, although business executives etc can still use coaching for self-actualisation its primary purpose is as a means of achievement of your proper employment role in balance and without attachment.

This can be illustrated by looking at Ken Wilber's specific ideology - 4 Quadrants of values. 105) Mindfulness is a part of Wilbur's Integral Life practice and balancing of the 4 Quadrants and this is not a neutral religious space. Instead it is a meditative practice, involving Body, Mind, Spirit and Shadow.

1. INNER SELF Self and consciousness "I"	3. OUTER SELF Brain and organisation "IT"
2. INNER GROUP Culture and worldview "WE"	4. OUTER GROUP Social system and environment "ITS"

There are 4 levels in coaching that fit with this model.

1. INNER SELF Non-directive Individual; Buddhist meditation; (balance -5 to +5) personal and spiritual (self actualisation / realisation).

2. INNER GROUP Non-directive Organisational; Hindu meditation; (balance -5 to +5) social (caste based, e.g. warrior and merchant).

3. OUTER SELF Directive Individual; Consumerist (pinnacle 1to10) personal (find ambitions, life goals etc).

4. OUTER GROUP Directive Organisational; Businesses and Monotheistic Religion (pinnacle 1to10) social (here there is resistance to non-directive coaching because people feel that it contradicts their faith, e.g. fundamental Christianity, or that it will remove their staff's ambitions and make them work only to a necessary level).

From this it should be clear that it is likely that there will be a diversity of sincerely held viewpoints in an organisation and the chance that everyone in an organisation would subscribe to a single system is slim. So the most promising way is to live with a diversity of viewpoints.

As coaching from the bottom up may have a limited effect (due to the variety of viewpoints of which the coach's is just one) perhaps the most effective way for coaching to create a change is if it is used by the leaders of an organisation.

Leaders' Use Of Inspirational Coaching

The role of the coach can apply to workers, managers and to leaders. However, it can be most effective in leadership. And in Ren Coaching Leadership is about having vision, which will carry you through times that a business isn't fully working. **106)**

"The secret for the coach is to create a compelling vision for people to buy into." To create a picture in the coachee's mind, asking "What will success look like, what will you see happening, hear yourself saying, feel?" "How does this inspire you?" **107)** This process can also happen for organisations.

One of the ways in which a leader can give good direction in a competitive arena, through a coaching approach, is to help people see their competitor as their co-operator. Wining is overcoming obstacles to reach a goal, but the process can be more rewarding than winning.

> "True competition is identical with true co-operation. Each player tries his hardest to defeat the other, but in this use of competition it isn't the other person we are defeating; it is simply a matter of overcoming the obstacles he presents. In true competition no person is defeated. Both players benefit by their efforts to overcome the obstacles presented by the other." **108)**

"Competition and Co-operation become one." And concern should be with the effort to win and not the winning. You can't control winning but you can control making an effort to win. You get anxious about things you can't control and this affects your ability so if your effort is for what you can control then your energy is more on task. **109)**

For the managers and workers to follow a leader there needs to be full trust and the leader must establish the need for upward feedback at the start of the relationship before any feedback is given. Ask if they would like it, and about what, and in what form:

"If I have any observations about you which might be helpful to you or your team, how would you like me to communicate them?"

"Is there any part of a specific task on which we are collaborating where feedback from me would be particularly helpful?"

"It feels nerve-wracking to give feedback to you: are you so busy/ tired/ preoccupied/ focussed. How can I best get through to you in these situations?"

"Would you like to receive feedback? If so, about what in particular, and in what form?" **110)**

The study of leadership is outside the scope of this book, however, an example of a detailed approach can be seen in the 9 dot leadership of the Power of Ren. It starts with the leader transforming themselves and at the end of the process they can begin to transform those around them who will become more willing to follow them.

1. Passion - the goal is set with passion that comes from honest self expression.

2. Commitment – from this there is commitment and focussed attention that removes interference. **111)**

3. Responsibility – we find reality with a sense of responsibility, aware of an interconnection of things and acting when we need to.

4. Appreciation – we have appreciation of all reality equally and not just seeking our own ends

5. Giving – our giving assures selfish return but we learn that selfless giving is its own happy reward. **112)**

6. Trust – when we give trust we relinquish control which encourages creativity and increases options

7. Win-win – from this position we can gain perspective to organise a way forward. With compassion a successful leader blends people orientated vs task orientated management. This leads back to the passion we started from, creating...

8. ...Enrolment - enthusiasm for enrolment (not recruitment) as we inspire by example and not by orders. The leader/coach inspires the ideals of the follower and turns these ideals into action, inspiring the follower to enrol others into the cause.

9. Possibilities – finally an openness to nothingness makes a space for movement. This is the detachment of the Buddhists and Taoists. Here

form is nothingness, nothingness is form. To be full is to be hollow, to be straight be bent. And for coaching it is to let go of our existing beliefs, views and judgments. For "Only when a person has travelled far and climbed high, will he be humble." It is out of this humility that we can be open to new solutions and plans. **113)**

This then creates a definite system that is, paradoxically, full of non-definite possibilities. It engages with what The Ren of Coaching describes this as nothingness but it could equally be seen as infinity. They are just two halves of the same coin, an open experiencing, beyond dualistic systems of categorisation. And this is the fractal FLOW. However, it is no good being open to every possibility except the directive one that your client / coachee might actually want.

So, following 1-3 on the Nine Dot Leadership list, new goals can arise and a new reality and responsibility be found.

This approach fits inside the non-directive organisational approach (2 in Wilbur's Integral Life system), which is hardly surprising as the Ren of Coaching comes from a Confucian approach that is focussed on the structure of society. And the authors of the Power of Ren consider that coaching is more Taoist and less individual, Buddhist meditation based. **114)** As such it is just one dominant quadrant of Wilbur's Integral Life, however, the value of its integration with the other quadrants is outside the scope of this book.

This Nine Dot Leadership can be mapped onto GROWFLOW.

1. Passion	G
2. Commitment	G
3. Responsibility	F
4. Appreciation	R
5. Giving	L
6. Trust	O
7. Win-win	O
8. Enrollment (Passion)	W
9. Possibilities	WR

so mindful balance GROWFLOW can be applied to both INNER GROUP organisations and INNER SELF individuals. However, in its pinnacle goal form GROWFLOW can also be applied to OUTER GROUP businesses and OUTER SELF individuals.

9. Conclusion

The key consideration is that there is no single answer that works for everyone, every organisation or for every situation. The successful coach is a guide who can help an explorer best if they provide coaching in a manner that is aware of its diverse approaches, its limitations and the difficulties they might present to different people and organisations. They need to be able to review and qualify the success of their approaches in an experimental methodology so that on the basis of their results they can adapt their goals and approaches to suit the participants and situations (whether individuals or organisations) pinnacle or balance.

The coach does all of this whilst maintaining a focus on the coachee and the work that they are doing.

J. Lynch quotes The Tao Te Ching as saying "With good leaders, when their work is done, their task fulfilled, the people will say, we have done it ourselves." **115)**

Going back to the start of this book. I mentioned that "the most important knowledge of a coach is that the coach should know themselves." This is so that they can know and work in the manner most suited to their coachee.

So if you find that being an instrumental / directive tool doesn't fit with your own coaching ethos, or that a coachee is seeking more meaning and cultural significance from your sessions and finds your directive approach too limiting, then you might find that another coach would better meet the needs of your client / coachee. And if you can move between roles then, to return to our driving and gardening metaphors, you might be called upon to be;

a vehicle - taking a person into a wilderness, a national park or a gardens, from where they must travel on foot, with their own map,
an adviser for that journey - giving suggestions on the best routes and short-cuts to travel, the best sights to see,
a gardener – helping the coachee's mind to grow and flower in its own balanced wilderness, freeing its rivers and waters to run unimpeded,
or even a landscape architect – planning and planting the wilderness, park or garden with a variety of flowers to grow and helping direct the flow of its water courses.

Happy Coaching !

BIBLIOGRAPHY

Downey, M., (2003), **Effective Coaching**, Thomson, USA

Eggert MA., (2001), **The Motivation Pocketbook**, Management Pocketbooks, Hampshire

Fleming I., Allan JD Taylor., (2006) **Coaching Pocketbook**, Management Pocketbooks, Hampshire

Gallwey T., (1975), **The Inner Game of Tennis**, Jonathan Cape Ltd, London

Garvey B., Stokes P., and Megginson D., (2008) **Coaching & Mentoring: Theory and Practice**, SAGE Publications Ltd,

Hall, L., (2013) **Mindful Coaching**, Kogan Page, London

Hughes, D., (2005), **Liquid Thinking**, Deanprint Ltd, Manchester

Jackson P Z., McKergow M., (2007), **The Solution Focus,** WS Bookwell, Finland

Knight S., (2006), **NLP at Work,** Nicholas Brealey Publishing, London

Landsberg M., (2003), **The Tao of Coaching**, Profile Books, London

Lynch J., (2013), **Coaching With Heart**, Tuttle Publishing, Singapore

Vickers A., Bavister S., (2005), **Coaching**, Hodder, London

Wilbur K.,(2006), **Introducing the AQAL Framework,** Integral Institue, USA

Wilson C., (2007), **Best Practice in Performance Coaching**, Kogan Page, London

Wong E., Leung L., (2007), **The Power of Ren**, John Wiley & Sons, Singapore

Articles

Grant AM., (2011), **Is It Time To REGROW The GROW Model?** The Coaching Psychologist, Vol. 7, No. 2, p118-126

Hawkins L., (2004), **Solution Coaching? No Problem! Part 2**, Industrial and Commercial Training, vol. 36, No. 1, p20-24

Megginson D., Clutterbuck D., (2006), **Creating a Coaching Culture**, Industrial and Commercial Training, Vol. 38, No. 5, p232-237

REFERENCES

1) Eva Wong and Lawrence Leung, *Power of Ren*, 2007, p.191.
2) Max Landsberg, *The Tao of Coaching*, 2003, p.200.
3) Max Landsberg, *op. cit.* p.91.
4) Garvey, Stokes and Megginson, *Coaching & Mentoring*, p.18.
5) Liz Hall, *Mindful Coaching*, 2013, pp.81-82.
6) Damian Hughes, *Liquid Thinking*, 2005, p.67.
7) *Ibid.* p.71.
8) Liz Hall, *op. cit.* p.77.
9) *Ibid.* p.120, pp.134-5.
10) *Ibid.* pp.144-147.
11) *Ibid.* p.186.
12) Tim Gallwey, *Inner Game of Tennis*, 1975, p.44.
13) *Ibid.* p.49.
14) *Ibid.* p.135.
15) *Ibid.* p.136.
16) *Ibid.* p.141.
17) *Ibid.* pp.25-32.
18) *Ibid.* pp.33-37.
19) *Ibid.* pp.50-54.
20) *Ibid.* p.37.
21) *Ibid.* p.85.
22) *Ibid.* p.138.
23) *Ibid.* p.113.
24) *Ibid.* pp.129-130.
25) Eva Wong and Lawrence Leung, *op. cit.* p.23.
26) *Ibid.* p.24.
27) *Ibid.* p.101.
28) *Ibid.* pp.171-175.
29) *Ibid.* pp.176-177.
30) *Ibid.* p.120.
31) *Ibid.* p.63.
32) Max Landsberg, *op. cit.* pp.54-55.
33) Carol Wilson, *Best Practice in Performance Coaching*, 2007, pp.116-117.
34) Max Landsberg, *op. cit.* chapter 11.
35) Ian Fleming and Allan Taylor, *Coaching Pocketbook*, 2006, p.34.
36) Downey, M., *Effective Coaching*, 2003, p.34.
37) *Ibid.* p.36.
38) *NLP at Work*, pp.218-220.
39) Max Landsberg, *op. cit.* p.97.
40) Downey, M., *op. cit.* p.63.
41) *Ibid.* p.187.
42) Liz Hall, *op. cit.* p.19.
43) Vickers A., Bavister S., *Coaching*, 2005, pp.71-77.
44) Downey, M., *op. cit.* p.191.
45) Vickers A., Bavister S., *op. cit.* p.85.
46) Max Landsberg, *op. cit.* chapter 7.
47) Downey, M., *op. cit.* pp.185-186.
48) *Ibid.* pp.44-45.
49) *Ibid.* pp.50-52.
50) Liz Hall, *op. cit.* pp.54-55.
51) Tim Gallwey, *op. cit.* pp.20-21.
52) Liz Hall, *op. cit.* p.70.
53) Liz Hall, *op. cit.* p.96.
54) Max Landsberg, *op. cit.* p.24.
55) Downey, M., *op. cit.* p.93.
56) *Ibid.* p.82.
57) Lynch J., *Coaching With Heart*, 2013, p.63.
58) Downey, M., *op. cit.* pp.84-91.

59) *Ibid.* p.146.
60) Damian Hughes, *op. cit.* pp.58-60.
61) Tim Gallwey, *op. cit.* pp.17-19.
62) *Ibid.* pp.57-61.
63) *Ibid.* pp.90-101.
64) *Ibid.* p.59.
65) *Ibid.* p.78.
66) Vickers A., Bavister S., *op. cit.* p.141.
67) Ian Fleming and Allan Taylor, *op. cit.* p.33.
68) Downey, M., *op. cit.* p.36.
69) Hawkins L., *Solution Coaching? No Problem! Part 2*, 2004, p.24.
70) Grant AM., *Is It Time To REGROW The GROW Model?* p.120-125.
71) *Ibid.* p.120-125
72) Vickers A., Bavister S., *op. cit.* pp.94-100.
73) Max Landsberg, *op. cit.* pp.30-31.
74) Grant AM., *op. cit.* p.120-125
75) Vickers A., Bavister S., *op. cit.* pp.109-110.
76) Paul Jackson and Mark McKergow, *The Solution Focus*, 2007, p.3.
77) *Ibid.* p.4.
78) *Ibid.* pp.10-12.
79) Tim Gallwey, *op. cit.* pp.42-43.
80) Liz Hall, *op. cit.* p.120.
81) Max Eggert, *The Motivation Pocketbook*, 2001, p.91.
82) Paul Jackson and Mark McKergow, *op. cit.* p.18.
83) *Ibid.* p.170.
84) Hawkins L., *op. cit.* p.23.
85) Tim Gallwey, *op. cit.* p.134.
86) Paul Jackson and Mark McKergow, *op. cit.* p.175.
87) Lynch J., *op. cit.* p.54.
88) Liz Hall, *op. cit.* p.109.
99) Max Landsberg, *op. cit.*
100) Downey, M., *op. cit.* pp.176-182.
101) Eva Wong and Lawrence Leung, *op. cit.* pp.189-190.
102) *Ibid.* pp.165-166.
103) David Megginson and David Clutterbuck, *Creating a Coaching Culture* pp.8-9.
104) Downey, M., *op. cit.* p.159.
105) Ken Wilbur, *Integral Life*, p.171.
106) Eva Wong and Lawrence Leung, *op. cit.* p.273.
107) Ian Fleming and Allan Taylor, *op. cit.* p.34.
108) Tim Gallwey, *op. cit.* p.123.
109) *Ibid.* pp.124-125.
110) Max Landsberg, *op. cit.* chapter 16, p.90.
111) Eva Wong and Lawrence Leung, *op. cit.* p.21.
112) *Ibid.* pp.236.
113) *Ibid.* pp.270-271.
114) *Ibid.* pp.23-24.
115) Lynch J., *op. cit.* pp.191.